Yesterday's Massachusetts

Seemann's Historic States Series

999

IVAN SANDROF

Yesterday's
MASSACHUSETTS

Seemann's Historic States Series No. 7

E. A. Seemann Publishing, Inc.
Miami, Florida

Library of Congress Cataloging in Publication Data

Sandrof, Ivan.
 Yesterday's Massachusetts.

 (Seemann's historic States series; no. 7)
 Includes index.
 SUMMARY: Brief text and numerous historical photographs, engravings,
and maps trace Massachusetts' history from the first settlement to the early
1950s.

 1. Massachusetts--History--Pictorial works.
2. Massachusetts--Description and travel--1951-   --Views. [1. Massachusetts--
History--Pictorial works. 2. Massachusetts--Description and travel--Views]
I. Title
F65.S34   974.4'04   77-23064
ISBN 0-89530-000-1

Manufactured in the United States of America.

Contents

Acknowledgments

I AM GRATEFUL to a number of persons who made this book possible.

A heartening assist came from the impressive resources of the American Antiquarian Society (AAS) in which I am honored to hold membership, and I thank Marcus A. McCorison, director; Frederick E. Bauer, Jr.; Mary E. Brown, librarian; and Georgia B. Bumgardner, curator of prints.

The *Worcester Telegram and Gazette* (WT&G), its publisher, Richard C. Steele, and librarian Sharon C. Carter were helpful, as were James J. Keeney of the Massachusetts Department of Commerce and Development, Division of Tourism (MDC&D); Mildred Prause, assistant curator of the New York Public Library (NYPL); Stephen Riley, former Director of the Massachusetts Historical Society; Dorothy Gleason of the Worcester Historical Society (WHS); Harriette Waterman; G. Ward Stetson of the Middleborough Historical Association (MHA); Marion Gosling of the Marblehead Historical Society; Herbert A. Kenny; Elizabeth Beston; Martha and Howard Sachs; Earle H. Sawyer; Annette Clark of the Ashburnham Historical Society; Ellen Mundell, librarian of the Merrick Public Library in Brookfield; Edward A. Laycock; Regina B. Munroe; Charles B. Everitt; Richard F. Leavitt; Amy Bess Williams Miller, and Lawrence K. Miller, publisher of the *Berkshire Eagle*.

I particularly thank my son, Mark Sandrof, photographer, for his technical skill and advice, my wife, Nancy, for much that doesn't show; Frank Close, who suggested that I do the book in the first place; and Broadus Mitchell, who read it.

Worcester,   Ivan Sandrof
Massachusetts

A WOODEN CARVING of the sacred cod, state emblem symbolizing the historic basic industry in Massachusetts, hangs high over the House of Representatives in the Massachusetts State House in Boston. (MDC&D)

Preface

MY INTENTION has been to bring out some unknown, or little known, information about Massachusetts as supplementary background to the considerable that is already known about the most storied state in the union. I have attempted to bring in such new facets in words and illustrations—the odd and unknown episode revolving about George Washington and two traitors; the most unusual hermits; the strange rocks of Massachusetts, some of her eccentric citizens, along with the old familiars.

Above all else, there are people—people mostly in the 1800s, fulfilling their orbit, working harder, demanding more, awed and fascinated by the changing scene, adjusting to new values.

The definitive work on Massachusetts has not yet appeared. The state is too complex, too storied, too large indeed to be confined. Anyone who has grappled with it emerges a little paler in the cheek and longer in the tooth. Something of how it is was told in an obscure regional work, *Historical Sketches Relating to the Town of Spencer*, published in 1903 by Henry M. Tower:

> Probably no one can realize the amount of work involved in compiling or writing history except those who have actually engaged in it. . . . James Draper says his history of Spencer would not have been undertaken had he apprehended beforehand the amount of labor required for its execution. Again, no man was so well equipped with facts in regard to Spencer during the Civil War as Luther Hill. He knew its history in detail and at the close of the War determined to write it. . . .
>
> For that purpose he secured a room on Beacon Hill, Boston, near the State House, where all the official records could be readily consulted. . . . He made perfectly sure that his landlady understood what he was doing in order to get maximum peace and quiet. And then, having hardly begun the work, but slowly beginning to realize the amount of labor involved in it, having health, time, means and complete data and resources at his command, he tore up what he had written, abandoned the project and returned home.

February 1977

IVAN SANDROF

THE BLOODY BROOK MASSACRE of 1675 is recalled 200 years later by this kneeling visitor in Deerfield. The settlement had been the northwest frontier of New England, pressing into hostile country and a favored resort of the Indians who called it Pocomtuck. A marble monument there explains further that "on this ground Capt. Thomas Lothrop, and eighty-four men under his command, including eighteen teamsters from Deerfield, conveying stores from that town to Hadley, were ambuscaded by about 700 Indians, and the captain and seventy-six men slain, Sept. 18, 1675 (Old Style). The soldiers who fell were described by a contemporary historian as "a choice company of young men, the very flower of the county of Essex, none of whom were ashamed to speak with the enemy in the gate."

[10]

THE FIRST PRINT known to have been made in the American colonies was a woodcut of Richard Mather in Boston by John Foster at age twenty-one in 1670. (AAS)

Strangers in a Strange Land

THE MOST INTERESTING STATE, greatest in achievements and the best known, Massachusetts is a fascinating study to any student who promptly begins to wonder how so much could originate from an area ranking forty-fifth in size among the others. It was the sixth state in the union, joining on February 6, 1788.

Thrust on dismayingly bleak shores with the salt Atlantic at their throats, strangers in a strange land, the newcomers were poorly prepared and trained for long, miserable winters and short, uncertain summers. The miracle of the first Pilgrims is that they endured at all. As it was, half died of starvation and disease. Others held fast with stubbornness and an unflagging Fundamentalist belief in the Bible.

The stiff-necks broke—those who refused to learn that food and fuel must be stockpiled in winter along with seed for spring, and that the occasional deer blown down by a blunderbuss was never there when most needed. This was hard to believe in summer, when the joyous green finally sprouted, brooks and rivers chuckled with fat fish, and hundreds of 25-pound lobsters clapped claws after every low tide.

Challenged to live or die, the settlers chose to live. To live was to adapt—and adapt they did with desperation that in time became Yankee ingenuity. Ice could last nine months, or more. Venison and other meat would keep on it, or stay blasted cold by wind. Certain vegetables layered in salt or sand and squirreled in a hillside hole might last until another year brought the crops again.

When food ran out, they garnered the last bits of the larder and even boiled leather straps to flavor soup, along with frozen carrot tops and twig ashes for salt. By then a rabbit might providentially hop in, entrapped by its snowy footprints. Sometimes an Indian appeared bearing maize, his stolid face glowing at the trinket in exchange. The stark life of the colonists helped to mould their character, which in turn affected much of what they did.

Long before all of this, in about the year 1000, the fabled Norsemen occupied Massachusetts for twelve years according to varied versions of history. There is some substance, but little documentation. But there is no doubt that by 1614, Massachusetts was being courted by England, France, and the Netherlands, with codfish as one of the principal lures.

John Cabot and son Sebastian made two expeditions to the North American coast in 1497 and 1498. English claims in North America were based on their discoveries, rumors of which flew from port to port where the important and profitable fishing industry was hard put to fill the insatiable demand from Catholic Europe.

Fishermen netted many varieties, but among the sweetest was the cod—easily caught, conveniently sized, firm of flesh, quickly salted in barrels or dried in the sun. So plentiful were they in Newfoundland, the rumors ran, that Cabot had scooped them up in baskets. It took hundreds of years before a similar legend swept the old continent—that gold was to be found in the streets of America.

Fishermen jerked up the stained sails of their bobbling cockleshells and pointed west. When enough were returning without falling off the edge of the world and with stuffed holds, hundreds of others were encouraged. How many arrived we shall never know, but we can assume that dozens of uncharted boats with their illiterate captains and crews were blown to landfall and plopped anchor along Massachusetts with its 750 miles of coastline and hundreds of harbors.

Among the documented explorers was Portuguese nobleman Gaspar Cortereal who led a small fleet to Newfoundland in 1501, sailed south to catch cod, and vanished. His brother, Miguel, arrived with three ships to search for him the following year, separated from the others, and created a Bermuda Triangle of his own by also disappearing. Other early arrivals on Massachusetts soil included Giovanni da Verrazzano, Estevan Gomez, Jehan Allefonsce of Saintonge, Diego Maldonado, Andre Thevet, Sir John Hawkins, and David Ingram.

The matter becomes somewhat academic if a report by Sir Richard Whitbourne in 1578 is to be believed. He wrote that 100 Spanish, 50 English, 150 French, and 50 Portuguese vessels were cod-hunting in a single season on the Newfoundland banks—and this only eighty-six years after Columbus.

Time brought organized explorers, with precise intentions. They kept more exact records, giving history a better purchase. Searching for sassafras, an aromatic tree bark "of sovereign virtue for the French poxe," Bartholomew Gosnold in 1602, with a crew of thirty-two, brought his bark to Provincetown. He scooped more codfish than he had room for, declared them easier to catch than at Newfoundland, and named Cape Cod with inspired inventiveness, brief, accurate, and colorful.

The expedition was profitable enough to bestir similar moves, the next only eight months later by Richard Hakluyt, with Gosnold's pilot, Robert Salterne, as assistant to Capt. Martin Pring. They beat into Massachusetts Bay, making landfall in or about Plymouth Harbor near where they found sufficient sassafras to stuff the barks *Discoverer* and *Speedwell.* The French got their biggest assist from explorer Samuel de Champlain, who in 1605-06 carefully mapped Gloucester, Plymouth, Eastham, Chatham, and the entire New England coast.

Determined to find a "Northwest Passage" through North America, the storied Henry Hudson paused briefly at Cape Cod in August 1609, giving the Dutch their handhold. It was strengthened in 1614 when Adrian Block and Henrik Christiansen in a jerry-built ship, the *Onrust,* charted the Connecticut River, Narraganset Bay, and Massachusetts Bay.

In his six-week sojourn in 1614, Capt. John Smith accomplished more for Massachusetts than all the other early explorers together. He became obsessed with its rocks and rills, and more with its codfish, softly furred beavers, and other negotiable assets, and for at least seventeen years diligently advanced the desirability of the area. "Could I have but means to transport a Colonie," he fervently wrote, "I would rather live here than anywhere."

One reason why the Indians and the English went to war can be seen in the actions of Capt. Thomas Hunt, who was with Smith on the exploration, but left to find cod at Cape Cod. He clapped irons on twenty-seven Indians from Plymouth and Eastham and sold them into slavery at Malaga, Spain, for twenty pounds apiece.

The plague that smote the Indians at Massachusetts has been variously called smallpox, measles, scarlet or yellow fever. More likely it was a variant of one of these to which the English were immune. So devastating was the plague, wrote Thomas Morton from Wollaston, that the living "would runne away and let them dy and let there be Carkases ly above the ground without buriall." Between 1615 and 1617, the population of Massachusetts Indians fell from an estimated 100,000 to 5,000.

One result was that the Pilgrims inherited some cornfields already cleared, and practically no enemies. How could they not praise the Almighty and believe without stint that He was on their side? After two years of digging themselves in enough to keep reasonably alive, the profitable cargoes bound for London were evidence of unlimited wealth to come. So began a reinforcement of new ships and settlers, including wives and children of planters already there. The *Anne* and the *Little James* dropped anchor in 1623 with sixty passengers. Some moved on, impatient for faster, more profitable futures.

A small colony under Roger Conant sprang up in what would become Salem. By 1627, it was successfully pasturing cattle, growing crops, and taking cod. The Salem colony got a boost from an economic squeeze in England that pushed many of the middle class into the Puritan party, which inflamed King James I to vow: "I will make them conform or I will harry them out of the land!" The harrying, continued by Charles I, pushed thousands to America in the ten-year great migration beginning in 1930 when Boston was founded.

In 1629 the Massachusetts Bay Company outdid itself by dispatching 300 new planters in six ships, along with sixty head of cattle and horses, and holds bulging with supplies. A year later Gov. John Winthrop arrived with five ships bearing 900 colonists for Salem and Boston. The Pilgrims of Old Plymouth were completely eclipsed by the incoming hordes and a pattern of growth quite predictable.

An unusual treaty with the local Indians that lasted forty years was established between Massasoit (or Osamequin), sachem of the Wampanoags, and the Pilgrims. Mutual benefits were spread to other tribes in southeastern Massachusetts. Visitations were encouraged, but without arms. White offenders were to be tried by Indians, and Indians by the whites. Led by the agreeable Squanto, the Indians taught Pilgrims how to catch a fish and hunt (they had come without fishing equipment), and helped to extend their fur trading. "We walk as peacefully and safely in the wood as in the highways in England," wrote Edward Winslow in 1621.

The death of Massasoit in 1621 at eighty-one began a succession of events that pushed the settlement of Massachusetts back by at least fifteen years, possibly more. The stalwart chief left his rule to a son, Wamsutta, renamed Alexander by the British. He died a year later as the long reign of amicability was deteriorating. Among other facts that the Indians were unable to understand was that they could no longer hunt on lands they had sold, and that they were being importuned to sell even more for baubles and bright coats.

Metacom (also Metacomet or Pometacom), a younger brother of Alexander whom the British had renamed Philip, and who had added the title of king to himself, inherited rule, along with the suspicion that the English had murdered Alexander. The way was opening for the most devastating Indian war in the colonies. Before it was over, several thousand were dead, including 600 Englishmen; 50 towns, mostly on the frontiers, were abandoned and destroyed, and 600 dwellings fired. A cost of 100,000 pounds for the war was later set by the united colonies.

The Massachusetts Indians were all but decimated, including the so-called Praying Indians converted to Christianity by John Eliot, the famed Massachusetts apostle. King Philip's wife and young son were captured, and the son sold into slavery. Philip was tracked down by the redoubtable Indian hunter, Capt. Benjamin Church, and shot by a renegade Indian on August 12, 1676. The powerful chief sprawled on the ground like "a doleful, great, naked, dirty beast," wrote Church. The body was quartered and the head taken to Plymouth to be stuck on a pike. There is no authentic likeness of Philip left for us to view today.

By 1650, the modest Massachusetts Bay Colony in Boston was a prosperous and powerful establishment with more than a touch of arrogance. It printed its own money; sent out its own troops to destroy Indians; ran a miniature state department to deal diplomatically with the French in Canada; and hanged, publicly whipped, or banished Quakers and other dissenters.

A dour fanaticism crept into the colonists' image of gray and black, a need to mortify the flesh. They objected to bear-baiting, an acute observer noted, not because of the pain to the bear, but because of the pleasure to the spectator. Much later, the Puritan ethic melded into the New England conscience which, it was said, "didn't prevent you from doing anything, but only prevented you from enjoying it."

A harsher view was drawn in 1699 by Edward Ward: "The Inhabitants seem very Religious, showing many outward and visible signs of an inward and Spiritual Grace: But tho' they wear in their Faces the Innocence of Doves, you will find them in their Dealings as Subtile as Serpents. Interest in their Faith, Money their God, and Large Possessions the only Heaven they covet."

Out of need and logic came the town meeting which became world renowned as an example of working democratic government. There were other remarkable milestones, including the emphasis on education. The founding of Harvard College, oldest in the nation, came in 1636, along with endowed schools and an edict of the General Court in 1647 charging selectmen to set up elementary schools in all towns of fifty householders. Those with a hundred were required to establish grammar schools. Such early beginnings may have been responsible for the founding of more schools and colleges of national repute than appear in any other state.

A New Citizen Emerges

MASSACHUSETTS was becoming too successful. The powerful London merchants trading the world began to feel the competition where it hurt the most—in the exchequer. Their laments reached King Charles who dipped his sceptre in 1684 to abrogate the charter of Massachusetts Bay in favor of a royal governor. Some annoying conditions were improved, but these worsened after King Charles died and Sir Edmund Andros was named governor of the new Dominion of New England. A council of twenty-eight influential men of the colonies was appointed to advise him, but his bumbling procedures inflamed the populace and led to his recall in 1689.

This act was most significant for the future. It gave Massachusetts—along with the other colonies—taxation with representative assemblies chosen by the people. The back of Puritan theocracy was broken.

A new citizen was emerging from the ham-fisted son of toil, one with vested interests in his land. He fed it with herring, seaweed, or manures, and it fed him—an arrangement that let him run it as he saw fit. The procedure made for choice, and choice made for independence and a concept of freedom eventually to inflame the imagination of people everywhere.

Only a year after King William III had signed a new charter for the colonies, witch hysteria struck in Salem Village. Was it the final clutch of the theocrats, aware of their impotence? Before the last elderly victim had cackled helplessly from her fetid cell, nineteen were hanged, and one man was pressed to death in Boston under dreadful weights.

In the American Revolution, the fighting from Lexington to Yorktown raged for seventy-eight months, but only for eleven in Massachusetts. Common belief all but holds that it was the other way around; of such importance was the rude bridge and the shot that was heard around the world.

Massachusetts had become increasingly angered by the Intolerable Acts—a popular name given to five laws passed by Parliament in 1774, four of them in retaliatory punishment for the Boston Tea Party. Attempting to suppress armed rebellion, Gen. Thomas

Gage, the British commander in Boston, acted on spy intelligence and dispatched a column of infantry to seize colonial military supplies in Concord.

At dawn, April 19, 1775, minutemen on Lexington's green intercepted an advance column of redcoats led by Maj. John Pitcairn on horse. Flourishing his sword, he cried, "Disperse, you damned rebels, disperse!" Capt. John Parker, commanding the two companies of armed citizens, ordered "Steady—now hold steady!" then ordered them to disperse, while Pitcairn issued a command ending, ". . . on no account to fire or even attempt it without orders."

Obviously no one wanted to shoot first; but some redcoat—never identified—pressed a trigger and the British discharged several volleys that killed eight and wounded ten. Minuteman Ebenezer Munroe got his in the elbow, swore to his cousin John next in line, "I'll give them the guts of my gun!" and fired what was probably the first American shot of the war.

Concord was next, with ragged engagements, sporadic rifle fire, increasing numbers of colonial volunteers hurrying in over the hayfields from Middlesex towns while the British were reinforced with the main garrison of Boston under Lord Percy. On the panicky general retreat to Boston, General Gage officially reported 72 dead out of over 2,000 troops on the march.

The Battle of Bunker Hill is shocking in comparison. The British suffered 1,054 killed and wounded out of some 2,300 engaged. Among the dead were Col. James Abercrombie of the Grenadiers and Major Pitcairn of the Marines who had lost his pistols at Concord. The colonials, under Gen. Artemas Ward, suffered about 500 killed and wounded, including the loss of Dr. Joseph Warren, a leading Massachusetts statesman and one of the most remarkable men of the Revolutionary period. The British had won a dismaying victory.

The spectacular achievement of the stoutly-built Henry Knox, a Boston bookseller turned skilled military commander, in dragging "a noble train of artillery" from Fort Ticonderoga over the Berkshire hills, gave Washington strength to reverse the British stalemate. In a classic night maneuver on March 4, 1776, some three hundred wagons, heavily greased and wrapped to minimize noise, and a working army of 3,000 men under Brig. Gen. John Thomas, crept to the top of Dorchester Heights, built almost unassailable defense of hay bales and barrels of rocks, and poked their cannon down to make the British position untenable. A Boston merchant had suggested that the barrels be laid so as to avalanche should the British advance.

Infuriated by the maneuver, Gen. William Howe ordered an immediate attack which was countermanded when a "hurry cane" beat up the harbor. It was followed by a decision to abandon Boston. Howe threatened to burn it if molested, and won a grudging permission to leave. After he left, gunpowder trails leading to piles of hay were found in various buildings. So were three-sided, needle-pointed, iron crow's feet, scattered at the last moment to inhibit pursuit, and spiked cannon, ruined supplies, and stores worth about 40,000 pounds. With Howe went his entire force of about 11,000 which included sailors and over 1,000 Tories, in ships stretched over a length of eight miles. The fleet, after several days of

ONE OF THE LESSER KNOWN early woodcuts of the Tea Party that shows the hard-at-work patriots masquerading as Indians and a large audience of Boston townspeople cheering them on.

SOME TEA PARTY TEA was salvaged from Boston Harbor by a witness with a good sense of history and later presented to the American Antiquarian Society. Not only was the tea dumped loose into the water but also the hatchet-broken chests. Much of the tea floated on the surface for a time before it sank or the tide changed and carried it out to sea.

[17]

EBENEZER MUNROE, believed to have fired the first American shot of the Revolution, left his walking cane for posterity. It is shown in the hands of a direct descendant, James Munroe of Miami, Florida. Ebenezer moved from Lexington to Ashburnham in 1782, and led an active life until 1825, when he died at seventy-three. A monument in Ashburnham's old Meetinghouse Hill Cemetery bears his defiant cry, slightly changed as too strong for the day: "I'll give them the contents of my gun!" (Regina B. Munroe, Miami)

PAUL REVERE'S ENGRAVING of the Boston Massacre is probably the most frequently reproduced illustration of the American Revolution. The original copper plate rests in the Archives of the Commonwealth of Massachusetts. Dozens of reproductions and copies of this print have been made through the years with various minor changes. Of the original prints made by Revere, at least thirty-six survive in the hands of institutions and individuals. (Alden Johnson, Barre Publishers)

readying in harbor, finally snapped a blue halyard under the Admiral's flag and slowly moved to sea and Nova Scotia. The war had ended in Massachusetts.

Historians at their own comfortable tempo continue to probe into the cause and effect of the Revolution. The entire history has not yet been written. One popular belief is that the Revolution all but took place overnight—but we now know that plans had been underway for at least ten years before by Sam Adams, James Otis, John Hancock, and other activists.

England cooperated unintentionally with a series of blundering political moves that spurred events inevitably toward climax. Today, the Tories enjoy a much higher esteem— along with the kinder name of Loyalist. Had they held fast and stayed, the brutal postwar difficulties might have been less and a readier transition made.

As it was, there were years of despair and near-starvation that soon followed the war. Inflation was so extreme that it drove law-abiding farmers in 1786 to march against the courts in protest of foreclosures for non-payment of debts. Shays' Rebellion embarrassed everyone. At the next election, three quarters of the legislature was emphatically voted out.

BUNKER HILL MONUMENT commemorates the Battle of Bunker Hill, June 17, 1775. The 220-foot granite obelisk, designed by Solomon Willard, is a nationally famous landmark. The cornerstone was laid on June 7, 1825, for the fiftieth anniversary of the battle, by the Revolutionary hero, Lafayette, and by Daniel Webster, who dedicated it upon its completion in 1843. A spiral stairway for the young of heart leads to an impressive view from the top. (MDC&D)

[19]

THE BATTLE OF BUNKER HILL by Howard Pyle is a careful and stirring rendition of what must have happened. Note the order of march, with the British officers protected by three lines of redcoats and the general behind the officers. The British lost 1,054 soldiers—over a third of their entire force—as against 449, or about a quarter of the Americans. (Wilmington Society of the Fine Arts)

VARIOUS SATIRES appeared in British publications following the famous tea party in 1774 and the blockade of Boston. "The Bostonians in Distress," printed on Fleet Street, London, was one of the best. It suggested that the rebels were being hoisted by their own petard.

THE RETREAT from Lexington and Concord of 1,000 British troops is graphically depicted in this contemporary woodcut by Amos Doolittle of Connecticut. A deadly guerrilla harassment by minute men from behind their stone walls, where they could reload at leisure, was probably more responsible for the 273 casualties than eyeball-to-eyeball conflict. The loss was three times as many as suffered by the colonials. (NYPL)

THE EVACUATION OF THE BRITISH from Boston on March 17, 1776—a day officially observed in the city as Evacuation Day, is the theme of this nineteenth-century engraving. Many cannon were thrown overboard or spiked useless, while loyalist civilians and soldiers were ferried out to every available ship the British could command. The only medal ever given to Washington by Congress was awarded as a result of this military achievement—a gold medal struck in Paris, showing Washington's portrait on one side and a view of him and his officers watching the departing British from Dorchester Heights. (NYPL)

THE BRITISH could not have been pushed out of Boston without cannon, then in short supply. These were provided by a Boston bookseller and patriot, Henry Knox, who offered General Washington a plan to bring ordnance back from Fort Ticonderoga. The journey of extreme hardship with oxen and horses was made over some of the highest mountains of Massachusetts. The successful venture led by Knox brought him the post of general of the artillery in the Revolution. This painting by Tom Lovell shows a reasonably accurate version of the "noble train of artillery" as it left Fort Ticonderoga, seen in the top left corner. The cannon were secretly installed overnight on Dorchester Heights, making British warships below the target of defeat, and ending the war in Massachusetts. (Joseph Dixon Crucible Co., Jersey City, N.J.)

On the Road from Annapolis to Queen Ann there is one considerable River to be pass'd, but as the Ships boats can easily be braght round from the Bay to the Usual place of Passage or Ferry, this is no impediment if the Two Corps chuse to unite They may by a single days march either at Queen Ann or Malbrough

"MR. LEE'S PLAN": Part of an eight-page, unsigned document in the handwriting of Gen. Charles Lee, second in command under Washington, was found among the papers of Lord Howe seventy-five years after the Revolutionary War had ended. On the final page, reproduced here, Henry Strachey, secretary to Howe, had scrawled "Mr. Lee's Plan 29th March 1777." On that date, Lee was living in elegant fashion as a prisoner of the British. His plan contained an operational scheme by which the British navy and army could subdue the colonists—a treasonable act. Had it been found earlier, Lee would probably have been hanged. (AAS)

AN AUTHENTICATED LIKENESS of Brig. Gen. Charles Lee is this contemporary British cartoon by Barham Rushbrooks. It was drawn on Lee's return from Europe in his uniform as aide-de-camp to Stanislaus, King of Poland. The dog was Lee's favorite, Mr. Spade. One of the oddest men of the American Revolution, Lee, as second in command of the Continental Army, was court-martialed and found guilty of three charges, but not for being a traitor, which it seems certain that he was. (NYPL)

STEARNS' TAVERN, its site in Worcester marked by this plaque, was where on July 1, 1775, George Washington spent the night. He was unknowingly in the company of two American traitors, an incident that somehow has eluded the historians.
(Guaranty Bank & Trust Co.)

Traitors Once Had
the Ear of Washington

A DRAMATIC INCIDENT on Massachusetts soil—an incident that has eluded the historians—involves George Washington and two American traitors with whom he was so closely confined a day and a night. That they did not try to brainwash him is hard to believe.

The two principals were Maj. Gen. Charles Lee, third in command of the Continental Army, and Dr. Benjamin Church, one of the most highly respected members of the top echelon of the Revolutionary hierarchy. Involved, too, was Silas Deane, a member of the Continental Congress and close friend of traitor Benedict Arnold.

Charles Lee, born in England, was one of the strangest characters in the Revolutionary War. Tall, lean, with a prominent nose and a receding chin, he was described as cantankerous, moody, given to sudden temper explosions, ill-mannered, a great sloven, wretchedly profane, clever at words, and able in an unpredictable way. His main attraction for Washington and the Continental Congress, which had given Lee his high rank (later he would become second in command), was his professional knowledge of military tactics, learned in Poland and Portugal. When the Revolution began, Lee was a British lieutenant colonel on half-pay who was buying land in Virginia.

Espionage was a way of life on the old continent. The French were traditionally skilled at intrigue, and the British not far behind. Kings had their spies—and spies, their kings. The royal courts reeked with informers sniffing up their sleeves, or exchanging signals in ballrooms where fans fluttered over rosy bosoms. And since anonymity and secrecy are the first rules for a successful spy, it is safe to assume that for every one exposed, there were others never caught.

The Americans also had their spy ring, established by Paul Revere and about thirty other skilled craftsmen of Boston in the fall of 1774 with the purpose, he reported, of "watching the movement of the British soldiers, and gaining every intelligence of the movement of the Tories." As the war fever quickened, the members "frequently took turns, two and two, to watch the soldiers, by patroling the streets all night."

The first oddity showed some eight months after the Revolutionary War had begun.

"Our cause has also received a severe blow in the captivity of Gen. Lee," wrote Washington on December 17, 1776, to his cousin. "Unhappy man! Taken by his own imprudence, going three or four miles from his own camp, and within twenty of the enemy, notice of which by a rascally Tory was given, a party of light horse seized him in the morning after travelling all night, and carried him off in high triumph and with every mark of indignation, not even suffering him to get his hat or surtout coat. . . . "

General Lee was at that point commanding 5,500 men in a critical military situation. What then was he doing in a farmhouse-tavern in Basking Ridge, three miles outside his own lines, at 10 a.m. on December 13, having breakfast and writing letters? One of them, to Gen. Horatio Gates, carried this sentence: "A certain great man is damnably deficient. . . . "

A scouting party of thirty dragoons—Burgoyne's 16th Light Horse which had served under Lee in Portugal—dashed in suddenly from orchard and woods, blazing at the tavern with gunfire. It was commanded by Lt. Col. William Harcourt, who had asked for the assignment. Also in the party was a Captain Eustace—an aide to Cornwallis who had come along for the ride.

Lee paced his chamber for fifteen minutes, then told his aide-de-camp to announce his surrender. He was tied to his horse and galloped away. The first stop was near the Raritan River at the home of a physician who was entertaining the British officers. One of them, a Major Moyney, recognized Lee as an old comrade and rushed out to embrace him. The dragoons continued to Brunswick, where nearly everyone proceeded to get drunk, including Lee's horse.

In New York, where he was kept a year and four months by the British, Lee was regarded as a most special person, with a sentry at his door. The door led to one of the largest and most comfortable rooms in the city hall. Lee was allowed guests daily at dinner, and his table was "very handsomely kept" by General Howe.

One of his early visitors, who came again later, was Henry Strachey, secretary to the Howe brothers.

Put on parole, Lee was allowed anywhere in the limits of New York City. Transferred to Philadelphia, he was even allowed to travel behind British lines. Part of his imprisonment included staying with two of his oldest friends in the British service and, in February 1778, he won a $500 prize in the Alms House Lottery.

Before leaving New York, Lee was a guest at a party in King's Arms Tavern. Lee wore a freshly powdered wig, a light blue waistcoat, white stockings, and gold epaulets. The party lasted until dawn. Flanking Lee at the table was Lt. Col. Harcourt who had captured him.

Finally released, Lee resumed his military command. At the Battle of Monmouth on July 28, 1778, Lee was ordered to attack. "But, strange to tell!" Washington wrote to his brother, "when he came up with the enemy, a retreat commenced."

The battle began with an American regiment turning back a British cavalry charge. Lee then ordered the retreat, but only informed the regiment next to him. Other units had to discover on their own that they were unsupported.

A furious Washington flashed in at the last moment to turn the rout into a victory. Lee was arrested, court-martialed, and found guilty on three counts: disobeying orders, misbehavior before the enemy, and disrespect for the commander-in-chief. It ended his career.

Only two weeks before the Battle of Monmouth, Lee wrote surreptitiously to both Howe and Clinton. When Clinton succeeded Lord Howe as commanding British general, Lee dashed off a letter of congratulations: "General Lee presents his most sincere and humble respects to Sir Henry Clinton. He wishes him all possible happiness and health and begs, whatever may be the event of the present unfortunate contest, that he will believe General Lee to be his most respectful and obliged humble servant."

Finally, and most damning of all, was a strange, unsigned document discovered seventy-five years after the war ended among the papers of General Howe. Strachey had scrawled on it, "Mr. Lee's Plan 29th March 1777." The date was three months after he had been captured and was a British prisoner. The plan was for the conquest of America by land and by sea. Had it been found while Lee was still a general, he probably would have been hanged.

The case against the infamous Benjamin Church, M.D., is absolute. He had worked closely with James Otis and Sam Adams as one of the chief architects of the Revolution, and was not only a member of the House of Representatives and the Committee of Correspondence, but chairman of the Committee of Safety which, at one point, made him the most powerful man in Massachusetts next to Joseph Warren. The plump physician was appointed surgeon general of the Continental Army, but became instead the first convicted American traitor—betrayed by his mistress after a coded letter had been tracked to him.

Church was imprisoned until the latter part of 1777, then allowed to leave for the West Indies, though not the slightest doubt of his guilt existed. He and the sloop *Welcome* were never heard from again. Family tradition says Church was thrown overboard. Another version is that the vessel and all aboard were lost in a fierce coastal storm.

Earlier, in June 1775, Washington had waited impatiently in Philadelphia for a week while Congress named his general staff—General Lee, Maj. Gen. Philip Schuyler, Col. Joseph Reed, private secretary; and Thomas Mifflin, aide-de-camp among them.

The day before they left for Cambridge to assume command of the Continental forces, Washington bought a light four-wheel phaeton and five horses from Peter Renaudet. a Philadelphia physician, with a double harness and a chair saddle among other incidentals.

Lee, Schuyler, Reed, and Mifflin accompanied Washington, whose six-foot, two inch frame suggests logically that Mifflin, the least in rank, rode in the chair saddle to provide more carriage room, and for security.

Reaching New York, Schuyler stayed on there after a round of festivities for the general and his staff. The others continued. There were stops for refreshments, one overnight at the home of Silas Deane, congressman from Connecticut, in Wethersfield, then a suburb of New London.

It was now June 29. The dusty, long-journeyed phaeton finally clattered into Springfield, Massachusetts, where two members of the Massachusetts Congress were impatiently waiting, with a mounted escort, at old Parson's Tavern. One was Moses Gill, a wealthy landowner. The other was Dr. Benjamin Church.

Church and Gill joined Washington and continued the trip to Brookfield. Here a troop of horse under command of Capt Joseph Chadwick "and a number of gentlemen" escorted the phaeton to Worcester for an unpublicized overnight stay at Stearns' Tavern, previously called the Sign of the King's Arms. There was a shortage of rooms, and the entourage slept on the floor.

Early the next morning, the procession left for Washington and finally reached Cambridge, from where Washington wrote to Congress of his safe arrival, delayed somewhat "by necessary attentions to the successive Civilities which accompanied me in my whole route."

Over four hundred biographies of George Washington have been published, but this incident when two traitors had access to the plans and the ear of Washington, appears to have been overlooked.

GIVEN at the Council-Chamber in Boston, *the Twenty-ninth Day of* October, 1772, *in the Thirteenth Year of the Reign of our Sovereign Lord* GEORGE *the Third, by the Grace of* GOD, *of Great-Britain, France, and* Ireland, KING, *Defender of the Faith, &c.*

By His Excellency's Command,
  Tho's FLUCKER, Secr'y.   *T. Hutchinſon.*

GOD Save the KING.

OSTON: Printed by RICHARD DRAPER, Printer to His Excellency the Governor, and the Honorable His Majefty's Council, 1772.

BENJA WHITE.

GOD *SAVE THE* PEOPLE.

WATERTOWN: Printed by *Benjamin Edes,* Printer to the Honorable COUNCIL, in House of REPRESENTATIVES. M,DCCLXXV.

GOD Save *AMERICA!*

Eleazer Brooks

GOD Save the UNITED STATES of *AMERICA !*

BEFORE AND AFTER the American Revolution: Official proclamations by the governor and top officials of Massachusetts changed suddenly—and remarkably—as this montage indicates. The faltering nation finally made up its mind after a fumbling start, and "God Save the United States of America!" it is. (WT&G)

ONE OF THE MOST FAMOUS SHIPS ever built, the *Flying Cloud*, here shown in a contemporary engraving, slipped off her ways from the shipyard of Donald McKay in East Boston in May of 1851. "She is, beyond a doubt, the most beautiful specimen of the Yankee clipper style of building, that has yet been turned off the stocks," enthused a Boston reporter. The clipper ship won world fame far greater than its value, for it was a race horse in canvas that caught the imagination. The *Flying Cloud's* 89-day voyage to San Francisco via Cape Horn was regarded as a national triumph—then she did it again, along with racking up 433½ miles in a single day, which was 42 miles faster than any steamer. McKay and his wife may be the two depicted at lower left.

To the Honorable the Council of the State of Massachusetts Bay

May it please your Honors,

With unfeigned Gratitude I acknowledge the favor you lately granted me, of a Reprieve. — I must beg leave, once more, humbly to lie at your feet, and to represent to you, that though the Jury of Matrons, that were appointed to examine into my Case have not bro't in, in my favor, yet that I am absolutely certain of Being in a Pregnant State, & above four months advanced in it; and that the Infant I bear, was lawfully begotten. — I am earnestly desirous of being spared, till I shall be delivered of it. I must HUMBLY desire your Honors notwithstanding my great Unworthiness, to take my deplorable Case into your compassionate Consideration. — What I bear, & clearly perceive to be animated, is innocent of the faults of her who bears it, and has, I beg leave to say, a right to the Existence which God hath begun to give it. Your Honors humane, Christian Principles, I am very certain, must lead you to desire to preserve Life, even in this its Miniature State, rather than to destroy it. — Suffer me, therefore, with all EARNESTNESS, to beseech your Honors to grant me such a further length of Time, at least, as that there may be the fairest & fullest Opportunity to have the matter fully ascertained — and as in Duty bound, shall, during my short continuance, pray,

Worcester-Goal
June 16th 1778 —

Bathshua Spooner

"SO PREMEDITATED, so aggravated, so horrid a murder was never perpetrated in America, and is almost without parallel in the known world!" Thus thundered Nathan Fiske, pastor of a Brookfield church, on the interment in 1778 of the body of Joshua Spooner, a wealthy, retired merchant of eighty-one. His wife, Bathsheba, sixth child of a noted Tory, Brig. Gen. Timothy Ruggles, was bright, beautiful, and headstrong. Her father had forced her at age nineteen into a marriage in which the next twelve years would see the birth of three children and her total disenchantment with her husband. One day she gave shelter to Ezra Ross, a wounded seventeen-year-old American soldier plodding homeward to Ipswich, and then also lured two British deserters, James Buchanan, thirty, and William Brooks, twenty-seven, into her barn, plying them with whiskey, money, and a plot to kill her husband by dropping him in a well. The four confederates were tried in Worcester by jury, and sentenced to be hanged. The prosecuting attorney was Robert Treat Paine, a signer of the Declaration of Independence. The defending attorney, Levi Lincoln, pleaded insanity for Bathsheba. Complicating the case was Bathsheba's claimed pregnancy, but a jury of midwives and matrons held her "not quick with child." Bathsheba then wrote a letter asking the court to reconsider, in that "I am absolutely certain of being in a state, and above four months advanced in it; and that the infant I bear was lawfully begotten. I am earnestly desirous of being spared till I shall be delivered of it." A second examination of "breast and belly" was inconclusive. On Thursday, July 2, 1778, some five thousand—twice the town's normal population—turned out for the hangings in the midst of a rainstorm. An autopsy revealed a perfect five-month fetus in Bathsheba, who was quickly buried in the garden of her sister's home. Bathsheba was the last woman to be executed in Massachusetts.

TIMOTHY RUGGLES *(left)*, father of Bathsheba Spooner, might have been almost the hero that George Washington was had he chosen the right side. He commanded a British regiment at Crown Point in 1755, was second in command at Lake George, and led a brigade in the Canadian expedition of Lord Jeffrey Amherst. As chief justice of the Court of Common Pleas in Massachusetts and a mandamus councillor, the highest advisory post in the colonies, Ruggles. born in 1711, lived wealthily in Hardwick on a large estate with sixty horses, prize cattle, and a twenty-acre deer park—shown above in a rare primitive painting done by an itinerant artist probably before the American Revolution. The Revolution split his life. When he wished to join the mass emigration of Tories and his wife and daughters refused to go, he sailed into Nova Scotia and exile with his three sons, never to return. For his loyalty, he was rewarded by the king with 10,000 acres of Canadian wilderness. Ruggles died in 1795. (WT&G)

THE DOOR KNOCKER of the Spooner house is the only existing artifact of a murder which the *Boston Independent Chronicle* called "the most extraordinary crime ever perpetrated in New England." Long since demolished, Joshua Spooner's house was close by a stage road then called the "old great road from Springfield to Boston." Dug out of solid rock, the well into which the victim was flung is now part of an old cow pasture near where the house once stood. (Merrick Library, Brookfield)

When All Roads Led to Boston

THE POSTWAR YEARS with paper money not worth a Continental, which is when the phrase began, created a seesaw of extremes that all but ended one way of life, and began another. Farmers slammed their barns shut and moved to better pastures in Vermont, New York, and then the Far West.

The early influence of Massachusetts on the rest of the nation is incalculable, for nothing grew as fast as the maritime trades. Massachusetts had the seaports, merchants, captains, and sailors—even the tall trees to build the ships and spar them. Off they scooted under wide-open canvas to hunt the whale, seize the cod, traffic in tea, silk, china, ginger, pepper, coffee, hemp, indigo, lumber—and slaves.

A most profitable trade with China began in 1787 when the Scituate-built *Columbia* was taken by John Kendrick of Wareham and Robert Gray of Tiverton around Cape Horn to Vancouver Island, then to Canton and Boston. It was the first American ship to round the wild Horn and the world.

The northwest fur trade became spectacularly successful, with repercussions all the way back to the farthermost woods of New England, where Indians got extra bright baubles for still more prime beaver skins. American imports at Canton went to $5 million annually by 1805 and were exchanged for ten million pounds of tea. Some profits reached $200,000 on an investment of $40,000. A high water-mark was reached in 1855 when Boston with 200 docks, handled 541,644 tons of shipping.

All hands, off ship or on, blessed Nathaniel Bowditch, self-taught mathematical genius from Salem, who corrected some 8,000 existing errors in current navigation guidelines and made it possible for ships to wing into port even when a snowstorm had obliterated landmarks.

Massachusetts was rich in many waters—sea, lake, river, and brook—with 390 square miles of inland water surface. The Pilgrims began using water power for grinding corn, called Gunney or turkey wheat, as early as 1628, then applied the waterwheel to the sawmill pits, easing their brutal stroking by converting to a crude type of power manufacturing.

The Congress-ordered embargo of 1807-08, which cut off essential supplies, and the related War of 1812 sharply affected the future of Massachusetts. What would soon become a vast textile industry was one of the decisive gains. All roads seemed to lead into the capitol city of Boston—the Hub of the Universe, the Hub, the Athens of America, the New Canaan, Mother of Massachusetts Commerce, the old Bay State, the Bay State, the Old Colony, the Metropolis of New England, the Cradle of Liberty, the Cornerstone of the Nation, the Greatest Irish City in the World, the Best Show Town in the United States, and Beantown. Some of the appendages were fanciful, but not the baked beans. By 1908, Bostonians would be chomping 33 million quarts annually—nearly 37 quarts per person.

Inland farmers, as far as the Berkshire slopes, shipped to Boston their fattest cattle, hogs, cheeses and butters, the handsomest D'Anjou pears and cheekiest Hubbardston Nonesuch apples. The pride of family affiliation was there. Many cities opened a "Boston Store," which by its very name suggested all manner of fashionable delights.

Augmenting early factory labor was the cottage industry—hand labor pieced out to the strong, deft fingers of women at home. It began as a stimulus to production when the General Court offered a bounty of three pence for every shilling worth of linen, wool, or cotton cloth. Later, boys and girls were ordered to spin at least three pounds of cloth a day for thirty weeks each year.

One of the more popular cottage industries, perhaps because of its flexibility, was the braiding of palm-leaf hats, sent south to shade the field hands. Barre in 1837 braided 607,000 hats worth $167,200, while Amherst produced 60,000, worth $12,000. Some stores took lengths of braided palm leaf as legal tender.

In Lynn during this period, a thousand women called shoebinders, working at home on pittance rates, unionized and struck. Employers sent the work to more willing hands, and the strike collapsed. The cottage industry reached a high level during the Civil War, when thousands of wives and children of soldiers made uniforms at home.

The inventors of Massachusetts changed the world. A partial list includes the cotton gin, the cotton mill, home electric lighting, the telephone, the telegraph, the sewing machine, the automobile, interchangeable firearm components, the digital computer, the space rocket, a shoe-manufacturing machine, a sprinkler system, a leather-splitting machine, Braille type, the adding machine, the cream separator, the drydock, platform scales, the hydraulic electric elevator, an electric fire-alarm system, steam heating, square paper bags, the power printing press, rayon, the motorcycle, and the continuous steel-rolling mill.

Massachusetts was first with the subway, the wool-worsted mill, the carpet loom, the refrigerator, the friction match, the pile driver, overshoes, rubber heels, the water-power turbine, the moving-picture projector, the fulling mill, the Stillson wrench, paper patterns, the steel shovel, hair clippers, and the machine gun. Include among these the first synthetic vitamins and the first birth-control pill.

The California gold fever struck hard in Massachusetts. In the spring of 1849 alone, 151 shiploads of prospectors sailed from Boston for the Golden State. The Civil War, to which the Bay State would send 146,730 men, gave another thrust to its industrial revolution. Half the Union Army pounded dirt on shoes "Made in Mass."

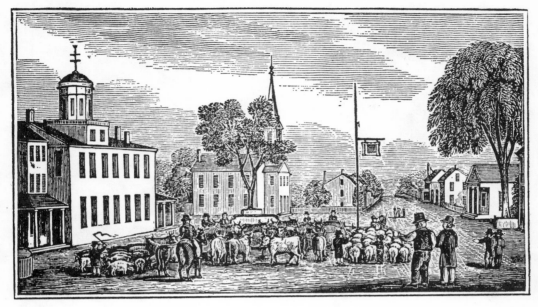

A THRIVING CATTLE BUSINESS in Brighton began during the American Revolution when contractors collected and forwarded their bellowing droves for the army. The market continued to flourish even after the war and became a colorful area of cattle, buyers, and sellers. This woodcut by John W. Barber, made in the 1830s, is of a typical scene. The Cattle Fair Hotel, at left, accommodated 500 on market days.

[31]

THE INLAND PORT of Worcester became a reality in 1828 when Blackstone Canal, a 45-mile ditch to Providence, Rhode Island, was opened with sixty-two locks and a drop of 451 feet. The first boat, the *Lady Carrington,* moved out with huzzas, a cannon, and two horses on October 7, 1828. Railroads ended the unprofitable venture in 1848. (AAS)

GUNPOWDER was originally so scarce and so unstable that it had to be stored in a very safe place, often on top of rocky ledges visible from a distance. Many odd and colorful structures for this purpose still stand in Massachusetts today. Most simply kept the half-barrels dry, and the powder was doled out to the local militia when necessary. But some were involved in larger events, such as this old powder house *(above right)* in Somerville, a forty-foot cone of fieldstone built in 1703 as a grist mill. On September 1, 1774, General Gage sent a force of redcoats to seize its 250 half-barrels of gunpowder. The incident provoked the Great Assembly on Cambridge Common the following day, when thousands of patriots assembled willing to fight at once. The same powder house a year later became the magazine for the American army that surrounded Boston. Other old powder houses include one in North Attleboro *(above left)* built in 1768; one on Powder House Hill in Amesbury *(left)*; one in Dedham *(below left)*, built in 1766; and one in Marblehead *(below right)*, built in 1755.

Straggling home from the woeful anticlimax of war, thousands of restless veterans sought a better life than farming stones in a depressed economy. They spread into far-off acres still free for land grab, where many would end in clodded graves, drained pale beside their wives by hardship and poverty. One only hears about the men who succeeded.

Smart, aggressive Boston money stoked westward expansion in railroads and mines. If hordes of Massachusetts residents left by the back door to settle the West, many thousands more poured in at the front. The potato blight had driven 200,000 Irish to Boston by 1875. The Italians came fifty years later. When the census counted heads, it found more foreigners in Massachusetts than in any other state except New York. The big three among immigrants were the French-Canadians, the Italians, and the Irish.

In progressive social legislation, Massachusetts has led the nation with many firsts: the right to vote, separation of church and state, the child labor law, legalization of trade unions, a state board of health, the minimum wage law for women and children, the first woman-suffrage convention, a state tuberculosis sanitarium, a state hospital for the insane, a school for the blind, colleges for women, the normal school, factory inspection laws, insurance regulations, compulsory automobile insurance, compulsory milk inspection, medical legislation, an employer's liability law, civil-service reform, anesthesia, quarantine, property-tax laws, vaccination legislation, the kindergarten, and a library in every town.

To this add the first missionary society, nautical school, physician, paper money, post office, American hotel, national dog show, apples (imported in 1629), and the birthplace of John Chapman, better known as Johnny Appleseed, who broadcast the fruit from Pennsylvania to Ohio for over forty years.

In its varied ups and downs, prosperity and depression, war and peace, Massachusetts reached superlatives of growth, claiming world fame for many of its cities: Boston, the leading shoe and leather center of the world, with a total annual product of nearly a billion; Peabody, the world's largest sheepskin tanning center; Gardner, the world's largest manufacturer of chairs; Athol, world leader in fine tools; Haverhill, the world's largest producer of slippers and low-cut footwear; Holyoke, the greatest paper center in the world; Lawrence, the largest textile print works in the world; Worcester, manufacturer of the most grinding wheels, leather belting, envelopes, valentines, corsets, and muslin underwear. And only by the abrasive products of the Norton Company of Massachusetts has that supremacy been kept.

The Bay State responded to World War I with the same patriotic urgency as in the Civil War. An estimated 200,000 men—83,220 of them draftees—went to war, with 5,200 killed in action or dead of wounds or disease.

When the war ended to the hoot and clang of factory whistles and church bells, so did another era. Hundreds of factories which had produced a third of the nation's woolens, along with a vast shoe industry, bowed to the inexorable laws of economics, moving to the South and the West for cheaper labor, more profitable raw materials, ease of shipping, and tax advantages. The great depression of the thirties blighted the land, and millions suffered.

It took World War II to roll prosperity back. While Massachusetts was sending 550,000 men and women into service and enduring 16,500 casualties, no peacetime expansion of

UNDER THE BANNER CRY of "Fifty-four-forty or fight," thousands had their war fever raised over the Oregon Question. War threatened between America and England in 1846 until news came that Sir Robert Peel was to be retained as prime minister, a move which insured peace. The news, of tremendous shock value, reached Boston first, where enterprising New York newspapers arranged for the quickest possible transfer of the news by train. Ginery Twitchell, a stage driver of Athol, riding horseback through a snowstorm from Worcester to Hartford in three hours and twenty minutes, continued his journey by train to New York, beat the time of the regular trains, and scooped the opposition. The daring feat was perpetuated in this drawing called "The Unrivaled Express Rider."

MERCANTILE RIVALRY between Boston and New York was extreme in the mid-1800s. Boston scored a considerable triumph when it became the United States terminus of the North American Royal Mail Steam Packet Company, founded by Samuel Cunard. The trans-Atlantic *Britannia,* pride of the fleet, flew its flag in Boston Harbor in January 1844, then underwent the embarrassment of being unable to leave when the harbor was frozen, a rare event. Merchants rallied, hired every available ice-cutter for miles around, and sliced a seven-mile channel to the sea. An artist caught the proud event, including the flag of Great Britain and of the United States, along with the huzzas of ice-cutters, merchants, and their ladies, as the *Britannia* began "to prosecute her voyage to England." (NYPL)

industry could match its frenzied march to work. Thousands of women flocked into beefed-up war production, making Rosie the Riveter a good-humored symbol of a new look. Few realized she was also the beginning of full-scale women's liberation.

Prosperity continued with the Cold War, but problems multiplied. Railroads, shipping, fishing, and agriculture went into serious slumps, but were offset to some extent by exciting new undertakings. New miracle fibers began to glitter from the old abandoned factories, and new and diversified industries created others. Farmers expanded into milk, poultry, cranberries, and market crops.

From the Massachusetts Institute of Technology and from Harvard, where the first digital computer yielded its readout in 1954, came significant directives to harness the traditional skills and brainpower of Massachusetts.

Hundreds of fresh undertakings began in electronics and nuclear physics. The Plastic Age, the Computer Age, the Nuclear Age, and the Space Age joined in a new dance called Rock and Roll.

To no one's real surprise the second largest industry of the state became tourism. Its historic shrines, Old Sturbridge Village, Tanglewood, and the Great National Seashore were among the leading attractions. The state had learned in pain that the only certainty was its glorious past, and that it would always be cherished for having given birth to a "new nation conceived in liberty and dedicated. . . ."

There is no end to Massachusetts.

A FIG DAY FOR BOSTON was November 22, 1851, when H. Harris & Co., auctioneers, bid off the cargo of the barque *Ionia*. Thousands of wooden cases and cylindrical drums contained Smyrna figs— the sweetest and best-flavored of all varieties. This poster is typical of such offerings, which were plentiful in the world-trading port of Boston.

A PRETENTIOUS COUNTRY ESTATE in Wellesley, created in 1852 by Horatio Hollis Hunnewell, member of an old Cambridge family who won wealth in banking and marriage, was later on opened to the public. The grounds were kept in exquisite formality in the Italian style, with pavilion, pine walk, and rhododendron and azalea gardens on six terraces covering two acres. A pretty lady with a hat fashionable in 1906 rests her parasol on a marble railing while viewing the pastoral scene over Lake Waban. (AAS)

JOHN HANCOCK'S HOUSE on Beacon Street, Boston, was one of the most elegant in the city, respected even by the occupying British during the Revolution. It was built of stone in 1737 and torn down in 1863 for non-payment of taxes, with many mourning the demolition of one of the noblest private mansions of the colonial period. The Hancock house served as quarters for General Clinton. Washington, Lafayette, D'Estaing, Brissot, Lords Stanley and Wortley, Labouchiere, Bougainville, and other famous names of their day were grandly entertained here. (AAS)

AMONG THE MANY Massachusetts political celebrities, one of the most memorable was Daniel Webster of Marshfield. It is not true that he once debated with the Devil and won. This daguerreotype is one of the best photographs ever taken of Webster. (Southworth & Hawes)

A MEMORABLE SCENE on September 17, 1859, when a bronze heroic statue of Daniel Webster was dedicated in front of the Boston State House, with thousands in attendance. Under the light-colored, striped canopy stood the spell-binding statesman-orator, Edward Everett, uttering his classic lines of "Liberty and Union Now and Forever—One and Inseparable." A year and a half later the Civil War tore the nation apart.

INDIA WHARF in 1857 was one of the oldest wharves in Boston. The cargo at right on the pier is granite slabs and barrels of whale oil. Note the cautious beginning of the age of steam with the single motorized vessel at top left. The structure on the pier sported a sign that it was a dining saloon, but apparently it had fallen on hard times.
(AAS)

"AMERICAN LADIES WILL NOT BE SLAVES" reads the banner on the right. "Give us a fair compensation and we will labour cheerfully." In the midst of a snowstorm, eight hundred woman operatives in the Lynn shoemaking industry joined a strike of firemen on March 7, 1860. The man in the first row of marchers is the chief marshall, so identified by the lettering on his high hat.

AUTHENTIC ANCIENT ARCHITECTURE is rare even in historic Massachusetts, which has more than any other state. Demolished on July 10, 1860, but leaving its imprint throughout photography, is the Old Feather Store, also known as the Old Cocked Hat, which stood at the corner of North Street and Market Square in Boston. The absurd names came from the old absurd hats. On the western gable was the prominent date, 1680, when the building went up after the Great Fire of 1679. Structured of oak, it was plastered on the outside with a slurry of oyster-shell lime, gravel, and broken glass. Two families lived upstairs. Two shops, the other a leading apothecary of old Boston, were below.

NOTHING LIKE IT has ever been seen—or heard—and behind it may have been the conviction that if it was big enough, or loud enough, the ear of God could be reached. The Boston Coliseum was built upon artificial land in Boston's Back Bay with over three million feet of lumber and forty tons of nails and other materials over a four-and-a-half acre site. Here was an organ built by J. H. Willcox & Co., vaunted as the most powerful instrument of its kind ever constructed. It was 30 feet wide by 20 feet deep and contained 1,786 pipes, the largest 43 feet high, supplied by wind from eight pumps worked by a gas engine. Here was the Big Drum, 12 feet in diameter and 5 feet wide, elaborately decorated by Lyford & Boyce. Here was the Orchestra, the largest ever gathered, of about two thousand musicians from all parts of the country, and from England, Ireland, France, and Germany. The basic purpose was to celebrate the National Peace Jubilee of June 15-19, 1869. From the attendance point of view, it was a crashing success, as this contemporary illustration reveals. (AAS)

A CLOSEUP of some early arrivals at the Peace Jubilee in 1869. (AAS)

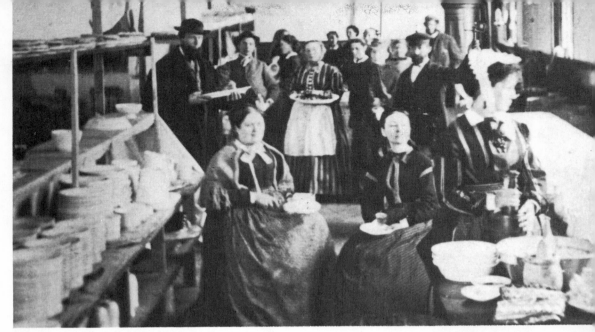

THIS KITCHEN INTERLUDE before dinner occurred at the 1870 Middlesex North Agricultural Exhibition in Lowell, which was attended by Governor Claflin, General Butler, and other celebrities. The proud-necked lady at right probably heads the committee of arrangements and is tasting the dessert. In any event, photographs such as this one showing the other side of the banquet are extremely scarce. (AAS)

THE HORSE IS MISSING, but the scene is called "Delivering the Mail at 'Sconset." That would be the village of Siasconset in Nantucket, the time about 1870. The women's dresses are striking, and so is the fascinating bonnet of the second woman from the left. The man in the wagon with the visored hat may be the mailman. The one blowing the horn is pretending for the photograph. What do you suppose happened to the horse? (AAS)

A RAGE FOR HEALTH led to a public interest in round houses that would let the sun stream in from sunrise to sunset. One of the first, an octagon, was designed by Orson Squire Fowler of New York, phrenologist and traveling lecturer. This shape had its greatest vogue in the Hudson and Mohawk valleys, but the concept also spread to Massachusetts where the idea of total sun appealed to the thrifty New Englanders—especially in winter. Fowler argued that his design saved twenty-five percent of building costs and avoided wasteful corners, as well as offering better distribution of heat and light. The design was even used for schools, churches, and barns. A classic stone example was built by Shakers in Hancock as early as 1826, and from it phrenologist Fowler may have developed his ideas. This 1870s photograph was taken in Foxboro before indoor plumbing was generally in effect. Note the number of outhouses.

AN ARCHITECTURAL PLAN of an octagon house in 1859 which could have been built for $1,500: A is the hall; B, the sitting room; C, the dining room; D, the drawing room; E, the waiting room; F, a dressing room; G, the greenhouse; H, the main stairs; K, the stairs to the basement kitchen. V and X are porches, and Z is a dumbwaiter.

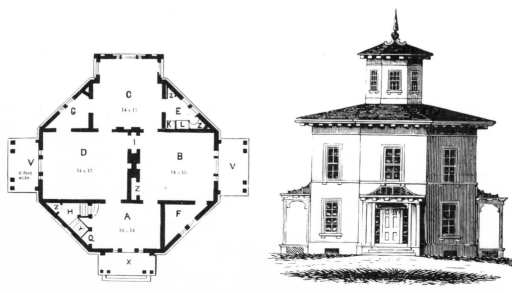

SOME BOSTON CITIZENS pause on the Common in 1871. The two bootblacks and their customers at center are artistically arranged facing left and right while another bootblack stands by and the moongazer with his impressive telescope-on-tripod looks over all. (AAS)

THE HASTY PUDDING CLUB of Harvard University lays claim to being the oldest theatrical organization in the United States and the third oldest in the world after the Comedie Francaise and the Passion Players of Oberammergau. Pudding, or Pud as it is affectionately known, was spawned in 1795 as a social club. "Society, sirs," reads part of the pledge of initiation, "is the source of the most delightful pleasures. By it the most distressing occurrences of life are effectually alleviated." The howling appetite of early students was effectively quieted in the old days with hasty pudding, a traditional dish of corn meal, water, milk, eggs, molasses, ginger, butter, and nutmeg, quickly prepared in a black pot over an open fireplace. By-laws still call for a pot at every meeting. Pud went on to theatricals and considerable fame with a famous roster of members, among them William Ellery Channing, Oliver Wendell Holmes, John Pierpont Morgan, George Santayana, Charles Francis Adams, Henry Cabot Lodge, Phillips Brooks, Alexander Agassiz, and Franklin Delano Roosevelt. Clustered closely in fraternity and fellowship is Pud, or part of it, about 1870.

[43]

THE LOCAL MILITIA parades over cobblestoned Main Street in Worcester, escorted by two drummers and an accompaniment of excited boys. This unidentified photo was made in the late 1800s on a warm summer day when streetcars were running but the horse was not yet seriously threatened.

OLD SPITE HOUSE in Marblehead squats on a ledge overlooking Little Harbor. Local legends differ on how it got its name. One holds that it was occupied by three fishermen-brothers in the seventeenth century who did not speak to each other. The second version concerns a summer hotel, the Fountain Inn, with an attractive view of the harbor. When a feud arose in the 1740s between the inn owner and a Marblehead resident, the resident is said to have raised a tall ugly house to shut off the view. Presumably, all states have feuds, but Massachusetts had a head start. The old town of Lancaster, then called Bride Cake Plain, for years held a lively feud between two men with adjoining pews in the same church. One built a spite-fence between the pews to block out the sight of his hated neighbor, but was made to remove it by church authorities. Feuds between brothers seem to be more violent than others. In Athol during the late 1800s, a strange house stood painted half-white, half-black. Two brothers who owned it couldn't agree on its color. Another house in the same town had a peculiar, unfinished look that was also the result of a feud between brothers. Unable to get along, one of them decided to move, cut off his part of the house, and left. (AAS)

The Old Spite House, Marblehead, Mass.

BILLOWING SKIRTS decoratively arranged, a group of women and two children pose near the top of Mount Holyoke in South Hadley, which overlooks seventy miles of the Connecticut Valley. A giant telescope is being assembled by a lone male to further enhance the view. The women could easily have been students engaged in a natural history field trip for classes at famous Mount Holyoke College for women, oldest of the seven leading women's colleges in New England.

BRADFORD FEMALE SEMINARY in Haverhill with a typical group of students, about 1870: Rolling over a campus of thirty-seven acres, the seminary was founded in 1803 as an academy and is considered to be the oldest upper school for girls in New England. It later became Bradford Junior College. (AAS)

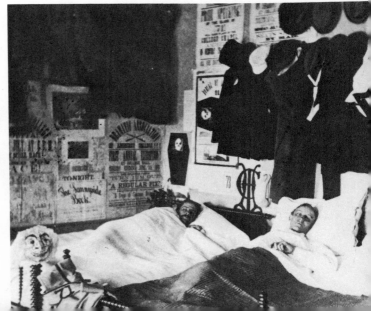

AMHERST COLLEGE—or part of the class of 1871—settles in for the night. The gentleman at left is already asleep and the other not far from it. High sleeping posture was typical of the day and considered better for the body humors and effluvias that infest us all. If the clothes hanging above the student at right are his, he owned at least eight hats, including the top hat on the first row at left.

THE BERKSHIRE BOY'S RETURN warmed the hearts of thousands during the Civil War and after, when it and other illustrations like it were popular. It depicted Charles Gates of Lee, a farmer's son who took the cows to pasture one morning and failed to return—until he brought the cows back from pasture after serving more than three years with the Tenth Massachusetts Regiment. Such humor, typically downbeat and Yankee, had many variations. In Nantucket a whaler returning after four years walked up the path to his home to be greeted by his wife. "Back are ye?" she said, handing him an empty bucket, "Why don't you get a pail of water?"

THIS GENTLE FIFER AND HIS DRUMMERS were former musicians with the Massachusetts State Militia probably celebrating a reunion at Gates House, Sterling Junction. From left is Foster Harris, who died at seventy-four in 1875; Daniel Hosmer, who died at eighty-one in 1879; and a third, identified only as Stuart. (AAS)

THE CATTLE SHOW PARADE, a frequent event in once heavily agricultural Massachusetts, had interludes of broad humor, such as this in the town of Shrewsbury in 1871. The horse with braids, pothat, horns, and wading boots nudged farmers where they laughed the most. (AAS)

ANOTHER ACT in the Shrewsbury cattle show parade of 1871 made sly, but good-humored jabs at issues of the times. Jim Fisk *(sign at upper left)* referred to notorious speculator, James Fisk, who financially wrecked the Erie Railroad, tried to corner the United States gold market, and was finally shot by a rival to the bed of an actress. The sleeping car, first introduced by George Pullman in 1859, was a good joke when added to the Dummy Railroad, a narrow-gauge trolley that ran to the resort area of nearby Lake Quinsigamond. The names Cabbageville and Flutterville are imaginary. (AAS)

TWO GENERATIONS have passed without once seeing the face of this lovely allegorical statue of Victory. She has stood at the top of a 49-foot soldiers' memorial on Worcester's Common since July 15, 1874. Prominent local men posed for the uniformed figures of the statue designed by Randolph Rogers at a cost of $50,000. (AAS)

A HUGE OIL PAINTING in Marblehead is to art what "The Battle Hymn of the Republic" is to music—a fundamental in patriotic emotions. *The Spirit of '76*, by Archibald M. Willard, is nine by twelve feet including its intricate gilded frame, and nine thousand visitors a year file into red-brick Abbot Hall (built in 1876) to pay it homage. A wagon-painter's apprentice near Cleveland, Ohio, Willard enlisted in the Civil War at seventeen, spending time between battles depicting scenes around him. When the nation made ready for a whopping centennial celebration in 1876, Willard painted a humorous Fourth of July celebration of a village center and named it "Yankee Doodle." A local art dealer saw sales possibilities and asked Willard to do it over with more spirit and patriotism. For models, Willard used his father—a gray-haired Baptist minister of seventy-four who stood six feet one—as the drummer, and Hugh Mosher, under whom he had served in the war, as the fifer. The third was drummer boy John Henry Devereux, who would later become a general. Two similar paintings, both in Cleveland, claim to be the originals, but General Devereux wrote a book in favor of Marblehead's version. (MDC&D).

LOOKING SOMEWHAT LIKE Civil War generals, the Massachusetts State Constabulary got together for a picnic at Walden Pond in Concord in 1872. Everyone is braced to prevent movement. (AAS)

A "CHEESEBOX ON A RAFT," the Yankee *Monitor* made naval history during the Civil War when it clashed with the Rebel navy's *Merrimack*. Their engagement was the first between ironclad ships and, while inconclusive, it began a tradition for the invincible engines of war that were to reach their zenith in the massive battleships and nuclear aircraft carriers of World War II. Clad in iron plates from three to five inches thick and one inch thick on the deck, the ships were used extensively in the Civil War, desirable in that they offered a low profile to the enemy, but with obvious unseaworthiness. The two "monitors" here, photographed at Boston Navy Yard about 1875, apparently are being repaired, for the guns on their revolving turrets near the bow are missing. (AAS)

AT A COST OF 195 LIVES, over twenty million dollars and twenty-three years of work, Hoosac Tunnel was finally blasted through the Hoosac Range in the Berkshires in 1874, saving travelers 125 miles. Four and three-quarters miles in length, twenty feet high and twenty-four wide, the tunnel is the fourth longest in North America. It began as a private enterprise in 1852 and, after much stress, was completed by the Commonwealth of Massachusetts in 1875. When the central shaft had been sunk to 583 feet, a tank of gasoline exploded, killing thirteen men. Their bodies were recovered a year later. This photograph shows miners lined up to descend the tunnel's west shaft in North Adams, which took the title of Tunnel City and the motto on its town seal: "We Hold the Western Gateway." (AAS)

CANNONBALLS in Ordnance Park, U.S. Navy Yard, in Charlestown about 1875: The yard, created in 1800, covered nearly eighty acres facing Boston Harbor and included three immense wooden structures under which the largest vessels could be constructed, a granite rope walk, and a huge dry dock completed in 1853. The frigate *Constitution* was its first vessel. The yard contained stores valued at five million dollars, artillery, anchors, and piles of shot neatly arranged and painted for preservation. The answer to why the Lincolnesque civilian is seated in the center of the cannonballs has been lost along with the name of the photographer. (AAS)

THIS WARSHIP tied up at Boston Navy Yard in the 1870s was the *Wabash*, a sailing ship in use just before major shipping underwent the vast change from sail to engine. Note the heavy Parrott rifles lined up to poke out through portholes, the furled sails, and the ringbolts on the deck to secure the guns in stormy weather. The massive guns still fired round shot. (AAS)

THE WHALING CENTER of the nation was New Bedford's boast for many years. By 1845 it had 10,000 seamen on its vessels, with record receipts of 272,000 barrels of whale oil, 158,000 of sperm oil—the best, and 3 million pounds of whalebone—much of it used in stays and corsets. This scene circa 1885 shows whale oil awaiting shipment after being unloaded on docks from the workhorse whalers stinking of oil, decayed blubber, and the residues of journeys in far places for four years or more.

CITY
PIER-2.

A VIOLENT ENCOUNTER with a sperm whale vividly illustrates the perils of whaling, first under-taken in the nation by men of Massachusetts. The scene, part of a panorama painted by Charles Ra-leigh, invokes an appropriate excerpt from the diary of Peleg Folger of Nantucket aboard the *Grampus* in 1761: "July ye 29 we stoed away our whale. We saw 2 Sloops to the Easterd of us, and we saw divers Sparmocities, and we struck one and maid her spout Blood. She went down, and their came a Snarl in the Toe-line and catched John Meyrick and oversot the boat and we never saw him after wards. We saved the whale!" (Old Dartmouth Historical Society)

[52]

ALSO IN NEW BEDFORD about 1880, when business was booming along the waterfront, two bearded men and prob-ably their daughters stiffly pose with barrels of whale oil in the background. The bark *Massachusetts* is drying its sails after returning from a whaling voyage. (Old Dartmouth Historical Society)

THIS SLEEK CARCASS, resembling an Italian racing car, is a dying 64-foot, 65-ton finback whale stranded recently by an ebb tide in Wellfleet and bleating helplessly in a primordial appeal. Cape Cod, hooking its bent elbow some one hundred miles to sea, is where thousands of such whales have been mired through the centuries, and nautical science has yet to agree on a full explanation. The most logical one is that whale sonar, or depth-registering faculties, are sometimes confused by an ear parasite during migration to southern waters. This whale died when the next high tide covered the blowhole from which it takes oxygen. The Coast Guard dragged the huge mammal several miles to sea, but the hawser broke. The whale sank until the gases of deterioration swelled the animal into a balloon; whereupon it rose, met the next high tide, and was washed ashore in another area where it produced a horrifying stench, offensive miles away until gradually ripped apart by wave, wind, bird, fish, and insect. Earlier, whales, called drift-whales, were given to underpaid Massachusetts ministers as a logical finish to what was obviously an act of God. (Mark Sandrof, Worcester)

ANOTHER FAMOUS SCULPTURE is *The Whaleman's Statue* by Bela Pratt in New Bedford, with its legend: "A dead whale or a stove boat." The spirit of Herman Melville's classic novel and its white whale, Moby Dick, still broods over this sea-washed community battered by economic storms. Tiny Nantucket superseded New Bedford as a whaling port, with 125 ships at sea in 1786, but silting of the harbor ruined the industry. Over three hundred islands in the Pacific were discovered by Nantucket whalers who raised the first American flag in a South American port, and who invented the first steel-headed whaling lance, credited to Hezekiah Cartwright. (MDC&D)

THE TWO WHALES here were being dismembered on the shore of Provincetown in about 1875. It was a race against putrefaction. (AAS)

FISHERMEN OF SIASCONSET in Nantucket in 1872 gathered on the sand to have their picture taken—and for the unusual occasion, donned collars and ties. (AAS)

A WHALE SKELETON, partial but including the spine, graces the front yard entrance of a captain's home in Provincetown in the 1870s. Two members of the family (lower center and far right) committed an unpardonable contemporary sin by moving and blurring the picture. The stone wall at right, unusual in an area where there are very few if any stones, was made from ballast off a sailing ship that was removed when there was sufficient return cargo. It could have been whale oil or fish, both plentiful in those days. (AAS)

[54] UNLOADING MACKEREL in Provincetown about 1870: The popular, tasty fish which ran in large schools was one of the mainstays of early fishing. (AAS)

THE NINTH LARGEST shipowning port in the nation, old Newburyport, with its vessels scurrying about the world, was a logical place to carry on an exotic bazaar. An aroma of sandalwood emanates from the photograph, along with suggestions of mysteries and strange, singing birds. The worldly, bearded sailor, the pretty young woman in her voluminous clothes, and the sign for Crofoot, the paper-box manufacturer, all add up to what could be a stage setting.

THE PROCTER BROTHERS Old Corner Bookstore at 123 Front Street, Gloucester, in 1874 featured a stereopticon (underneath the large gaslight fixture) with views of Cape Ann scenery that included the old fishing port of Gloucester. Here you could buy secondhand books cheap or rent from Procter's Popular Library at two cents per day.

WHAT AN INTERESTING INTERIOR the Oriental Tea Company had when it was graced by dragons and illuminated by gas. Here Boston came for its choice teas—Boheas, Lapsangs, or Oolongs, flown in on the windsails of China clippers. On Court Street in the old Scollay Square section of the city, the emporium for nearly a century advertised with a giant, steaming tea kettle hung over its entrance. The company offered forty pounds of tea to the first person guessing its capacity. Some 15,000 attended the moment of truth in 1847 when the lid was removed. Out popped a small boy, followed by a second, third, fourth, fifth, sixth, seventh, and eighth. Then came a man wearing a tall silk hat. The capacity, correctly guessed by eight out of 13,000 submissions, was 227 gallons, two quarts, one pint, and three gills. The newspapers called it Boston's Second Tea Party. (AAS)

THE 5-CENT CIGAR, a sociological butt of humor, really existed, and here is proof in the window of the Gem Cigar Store at 239 Hanover Street, Boston. Was the pail beside the gaslight for spitters? (AAS)

PRESIDENT ULYSSES S. GRANT and a party visited the Camp Ground of Martha's Vineyard on August 31, 1874, as the guests of Bishop Haven on Clinton Avenue. Leaning on the President is his wife, Julia. At left is Gen. Orville E. Babcock, the President's private secretary who was implicated in graft scandals but escaped punishment. The others are Mrs. Babcock, Miss Campbell, Mrs. Babcock's sister, and a Miss Barnes, otherwise unidentified. (AAS)

OIL LAMPS and horsehair furniture mark the living room of an unidentified mansion in Gardner, probably the home of an early chair manufacturer. The time is about 1875. (AAS)

THIS BOSTON WATERFRONT scene was engraved by E. P. Brandard in 1872. Steam has not yet replaced sails, but there is a portent in the paddlewheeler seen in the distance at far right. The ladle on the wheelbarrow in the right foreground was used when sealing the seams in ship's planking. (NYPL)

[58]

BY 1877 BRIGHTON had a new $400,000 abbatoir on fifty acres situated so that sloops and schooners could approach its wharf to carry on their business in small waters. The photograph shows cattle in pens that are conveniently near the railroad. (AAS)

A PANORAMA OF EAST BOSTON, about 1875, from the top of Bunker Hill Monument in Charlestown, which became part of Boston in 1874: The Boston Navy Yard runs along the shore. The prominent warship, old style, is the *Ohio* of seventy-four guns. It was used here as a receiving ship, with artificial rig for decoration only. Note at left the water pits for seasoning timber designed for use in ships. Across the water is Noddle's Island, which shared in the expansion of East Boston as one of the great shipbuilding centers of the world. (AAS)

[59]

HARVESTING ICE was once a thriving industry in Massachusetts when ingenious farmers found that slabs of ice put together and generously covered with sawdust would last well into the summer. Here is Salisbury Pond in Worcester with the industry in full swing on January 22, 1895. (AAS)

A LARGE FORTUNE IN ICE, beginning in 1805, was made by Frederick Tudor of Boston who won the name of the Ice King. He began his profitable trade with the West Indies and later expanded to South America and the Far East, bartering ice for return loads of linseed, shellac, indigo, saltpeter, jute, and even gunny sacks. Tudor bought a stately mansion on Beacon Street and, like many other large-fleeted shipowners, took pleasure in watching his ships come in. The size of the cargo could be estimated by how low the ship rode and how she handled. This is Tudor's wharf in about 1875 at Charlestown from where much of his cold cargo was shipped. In the foreground is the *Jean Ingelow*. (AAS)

THE BEST-KNOWN STATUE in Massachusetts is *The Minute Man,* by David Chester French, which marks one of the focal points of the American Revolution in Concord. It was unveiled at the centennial of the battle of Concord by Ralph Waldo Emerson, with an impressive audience that included President U. S. Grant. French, then only twenty-five. was in Italy working on a new statue. *The Minute Man* was his first. Too poor to hire a model, he draped a statue of the Apollo Belvedere with the trappings of a Colonial farmer-fighter. (MDC&D)

A SCENIC HARRINGTON CORNER, Worcester, in the 1880s, with cars of the Worcester Horse Railroad and a plenitude of stanchions to curb a horse or to lean against. (AAS)

SUMMERTIME—and school's out. Lincoln's Store, much the same as it always was, dreams on in the center of Southville, with the town pump still functioning in case your own well runs out of water. All that's missing is a hound dog with fleas to accompany the boys.

BANCROFT TOWER, donated by a philanthropist to honor a native son, George Bancroft—secretary of the Navy, founder of Annapolis, statesman, and historian—rises from the top of one of the loftiest sites in Worcester. It was designed by McKim, Reid & White, famous nineteenth-century architects. With so much stone on hand—and free—many Massachusetts buildings were built of it or had stone foundations. (AAS)

ANOTHER FIELDSTONE TOWER, in Lake Park, Worcester, marked the site of the Lenorson home from where, in 1695, Samuel Lenorson, twelve, was seized by Indians. Two years later he was with his Indian master at the burning of Haverhill, and helped Hannah Dustin, folk heroine, to escape after killing her captors. (AAS)

A RICH STRIKE in mastodon teeth took place in Northboro in 1884 when the hired hands of farmer William U. Maynard were digging a drainage ditch in a hayfield and clunked against some teeth fifteen times larger than that of a horse or cow. The teeth were pronounced to be the authentic remains of *Mastodon americanus* by Harvard's Museum of Comparative Zoology. Intensified digging revealed no more teeth, but a brown human skull eighteen feet away. Rumors of an early folktale about a murdered traveling man appeared, and the *Clinton Courant* asked pointed questions: "Did the man kill the mastodon, or did the mastodon kill the man? If the man first killed the beast, what destroyed the man? If the beast first killed the man, what destroyed the beast?, or was it an 'affair of honor,' fatal to both biped and quadruped? Did either slip in that Northboro pasture, fall, strike a Northboro boulder and break his neck in an attempt to annihilate his adversary—and if so, who and which?" Harvard ruled that the skull was that of an Indian female, not long in the peat and of no association with the mastodon.

[63]

THIS VICTORIAN MANSION in Athol was built by Addison Sawyer, a wealthy resident who invented the Sawyer canister, an exploding shell, during the Civil War. He also invented a meat-chopper and, with two other mechanics who were brothers, invented a cane-splitting machine that soon dumped reed and rattan furniture around the world at a fraction of its previous cost. His mansion was replaced by a hospital in the 1940s.

THIS DEPOT RESTAURANT in Ayer Junction, Massachusetts, in the late 1800s still depended on hanging oil lamps. The unusual white object rising from the large container on the counter may be a large block of ice that is cooling beer. Note how all of the subjects "froze" for the picture.

AN OUTPOURING of patriotism in the Civil War had sent a disproportionate number of men into service. As evidenced in a one-hundred-fiftieth-anniversary float, the town of Northboro with a population of 1,500, had furnished 143 men for the Civil War. (AAS)

THE YOUNG PEOPLE'S Society of Christian Endeavor flocked into Boston for a week of convention in 1895. They gathered to pray in tents, and strolled the city with dedicated gaiety, their faces radiating the pledge of the organization "to fulfill an earnest Christian life among its members, to promote their mutual acquaintance, and to make them more useful servants of God." Meanwhile, the Moxie company, knowing youth's affinity with thirst, erected the huge bottle that looms at left center in front of the tent.

INDUSTRIAL ACCIDENTS, many fatal, were caused during the great industrial expansion when flailing machinery and power belts whirled only inches from the operators. This typical scene of an open factory floor was in the Putnam Machine Company shop in Fitchburg. Such conditions led to stringent inspections and safety laws, which Massachusetts was the first to adopt. (AAS)

A NEW TRANSPORTATION ERA DAWNS: The first automobiles to come to Worcester, second largest city in Massachusetts, had their pictures taken before the Locomobile Company agency in 1898. The horse, however, was still undeniably king of the street, judging from the debris on the cobblestones between the streetcar tracks. Left and right had not yet been differentiated for the snorting buggies that preferred gasoline to oats.

DEATH OF A PRESIDENT: William McKinley, 25th president of the United States, was mourned in Boston in 1901 when, along with other prominent structures, the leading mercantile establishment of Jordan Marsh was heavily draped in black around a huge painting of the president. Mourning in this fashion has gone out of style here, but is still in favor in Europe and Asia, particularly in the USSR and in China. (AAS)

PRESIDENT THEODORE ROOSEVELT came to Worcester in 1902 to address the first graduating class of Clark University. He also appeared at the local fair grounds before veterans of the Grand Army of the Republic. "You are to be congratulated, not pitied, that you had infinitely difficult work," he said. (AAS)

PRESIDENT ROOSEVELT was formally escorted to lunch at the home of Sen. George Frisbie Hoar, shown beside him to his left in the middle seat. Driving the four-in-hand is Harry Worcester Smith, a prominent Worcester-area horseman who won fame by turning a milk-wagon plug into a sweepstake winner. Beside him is a Secret Service agent. The mounted escort at right was traditional and was provided for dignitaries all the way back to Washington, with each town providing its own escort from the beginning to the end of its boundaries. (WHS)

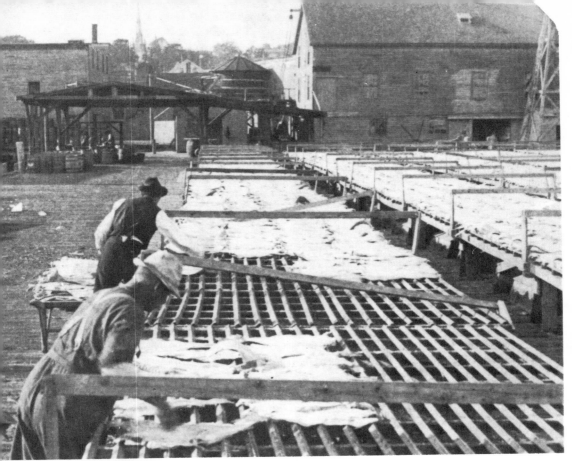

A REDOLENT ODOR of drying fish was as natural to residents of fishing towns as the sea tang it mingled with. Large cod were filleted and spread out to dry in the sun on open rocks, or drying flakes, as they were called. This particular process has long been abandoned. The scene shows cod from the Grand Banks being spread on the flakes of Gloucester in 1903. (AAS)

THE RUNNING OF ALEWIVES, or herring, from ocean to freshwater ponds to spawn, was an early spring event of importance to the local economy. Among the best known was the run at East Taunton, where fishermen are shown preparing to net the herring that are thrusting upstream, propelled by still not fully understood forces of nature. (AAS)

THE GALA LUNCH CART of Franklin's Cafe sparkled in the early 1900s with circus-wagon art and handsome red-and-white windows inset with portraits of Columbus, Pocahontas, and Presidents Washington, Taft, Garfield, and Grant, among others. The straw-hatted owner put on a fresh collar and tie for this picture taken in or near Worcester, which claims to have originated the popular lunch cart. (Frank E. Gaudette, East Brookfield)

A VAST INFLUX of Italian immigrants in the early 1900s turned Boston's North End into one of the most congested areas of any major American city. In metropolitan Boston, the largest number of foreign-born came from Canada, followed in order by those from Ireland, Italy, Russia, and the United Kingdom. Boston police on horseback patroled the cobblestoned streets, as in this happy 1905 scene in which an officer and his horse are making friends with a trick dog, a multitude of children, and some mothers. (Orville C. Rand, Boston)

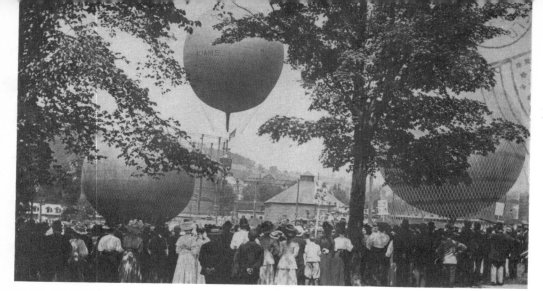

THE BALLOON RACE AT NORTH ADAMS about 1905 was a highlight in an era that had few such diversions. The balloons probably got their lift from the gas works, shown to the right of the balloon on the ground. (AAS)

THE BALLOON "Boston," carrying Charles F. Glidden and J. Walter Flagg, rises from Framingham on May 4, 1909. Note the new five-decker, built quickly to answer a need for inexpensive housing in an area bursting with the industrial revolution. (AAS)

AN EARLY AERIAL BARNSTORMER who thrilled the populace at county fairs was A. Roy Knabenshue and his air ship. The flight shown was at the Brockton County Fair in 1905. It's difficult to believe that this crude "potato" flew—but fly it did. (AAS)

THE TYPICAL RAILROAD STATION in any lively American city was one of the most exciting places, huffing and puffing with smoke and the smell of cinders, and roaring and hissing with steam, metal on metal, and the cry of conductors. Here is Greenfield, a gateway to western Massachusetts, about 1905. (AAS)

THIS LOBSTERMAN'S SHACK in Rockport, typical of those in most Massachusetts seaports, is an exhibit of orderly confusion as well as of a highly profitable business that is tightly controlled by Maine marketing groups. The slatted boxes at right are traditional lobster traps, while the wooden buoys hanging on the shack are used to locate the traps. Lobstermen use individual markings and colors on their buoys for easy recognition. (MDC&D)

FIGHTING FOR ITS LIFE earlier this century, a decaying apple tree matches the mood of an old New England homestead slowly returning to the soil. The Fuller-Trask-Davidson place in West Millbury was built by farmers in 1743—thirty-two years before the American Revolution. The chimney was of imported English brick, probably brought over as ballast. The house was put to the torch in 1956 as a public menace. (WT&G)

THE SAME HOUSE is shown here when roses were in bloom—about 1900.

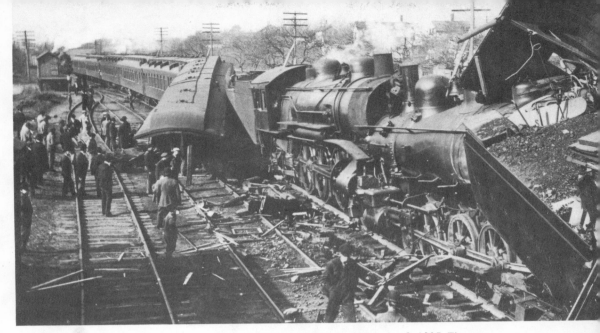

A HEAD-ON COLLISION of two trains occurred in West Brookfield on November 9, 1907. The engines were still huffing smoke when the photographer set up his tripod. (AAS)

MASSACHUSETTS WAS HOST in the only American appearance of Sigmund Freud, father of psychoanalysis. He attended a week-long seminar at Clark University in Worcester in 1909, along with some of the world's most distinguished psychologists. Freud is at left in the front row with the president of Clark, G. Stanley Hall (center), who brought him to Worcester, and C. G. Jung. In back, from the left, are A. A. Brill, Ernest Jones, and Sandor Ferenczi. Note the cigar in Freud's left hand on the cane. His inveterate cigar smoking led to cancer of the jaw, from which he died in 1939. (Clark University)

WILLIAM HOWARD TAFT, 27th President of the United States, leaving Mechanics Hall, Worcester, on April 3, 1910, after addressing the Train Service Men's Association: A Secret Service man is at left. (AAS)

HOMAGE TO PRESIDENT TAFT included a magnificent parade—old style, curb to curb—featuring four companies of militia and a battalion of artillery. The point-man at lower left seems intent on splitting the spectator, an illusion emphasized by the camera angle. (AAS)

AN EXCITING NEW ERA for motorists was opened in western Massachusetts when the Mohawk Trail, built at a cost of $368,000, was dedicated on October 27, 1914. The wildly inclined area, previously inaccessible because of extreme grades, formed the connecting link between the Massachusetts highway from Boston to New York. Millions have driven it for the annual glory of the autumn leaves. This thrilling hairpin turn was the sensation of Massachusetts motorists less than three years after the road was completed. Sightseers, including those on the first Albany-to-Boston bus to pass through, pause for the camera. (Lewis Canedy)

IT'S JULY IN 1910 in the town of Middleboro, and wealthy citizen Jesse Morse takes his wife, Alberta, and her sister out for a spin. (MHA)

THE CAPE COD CANAL, completed shortly before World War I and later enlarged to a 32-foot depth and 500-foot width, had been considered since 1697 when the General Court of Massachusetts ordered a survey made on the possibilities of a canal across the Cape. It provides a shorter and safer passage by about one-hundred-forty miles from Boston to Long Island Sound, eliminating the hazard of shallow waters off Provincetown. Completion of the canal made an island of Cape Cod, strictly speaking. The photograph taken about 1913 shows the dredge *Governor Warfield* at work in the draw of Bourne Bridge. (AAS)

[75]

The Smallest Steam Engine
IN THE WORLD.
Constructed by - D. A. A. BUCK.
WORCESTER, MASS.

THE MASSACHUSETTS INGENUITY that created so much occasionally took a change of pace, and if the first, or the largest of something—like a great cheese for the President—could command attention, so could the smallest. In Worcester, watchmaker and jeweler D. A. A. Buck built the smallest steam engine in the world, and it whirled, hissed, and spat like an angry mosquito. Engine, boiler, governor, and pumps stood in a space seven-sixteenths of an inch square and five-eighths of an inch high, containing 148 distinct parts fastened together with 52 screws, the smallest about a one-hundredth of an inch. All the bearings had standard turned oil cups. The boiler, using three drops of water, was supplied with a safety valve. Mechanics everywhere shook their heads in wonder.

[76]

THE INNOCENCE of ignorance lies in these happy faces of World War I, taken in 1917 in a YMCA building at Camp Devens. Still unaware of 333,182 casualties to come, including a number in their own group, they represented part of the first selective service inductees attached to the 301st Infantry. Their first uniform had old-issue canvas leggings, later discarded for woolen khaki spiral puttees that wrapped around the legs like a bandage. (AAS)

CAMP DEVENS—later Fort Devens—in Ayer sprouted almost overnight from 10,000 scrub acres to an important federal encampment or training cantonment for the American Expeditionary Force of World War I in 1917. Over 100,000—many from other states—were trained here. In World War II, in the Korean conflict, and in the Vietnam war, Devens was one of the leading eastern induction centers. Between the two major wars it was home to the 13th Infantry and also held the 66th Infantry, a pioneer light-tank outfit. The name honored Gen. Charles Devens (1820-91), a Massachusetts native and Civil War hero. The photograph shows World War I soldiers writing home during an interlude. (AAS)

MANES TOSSING, three fire horses faithfully deliver Ladder 3 of the Boston Fire Department. The year is 1919 (Orville C. Rand, Boston)

A VIEW OF ADAMS from the east showing Mount Greylock which has an altitude of 3,505 feet, the highest mountain in Massachusetts: Adams was split into Adams and North Adams a hundred years after its incorporation in 1778. At the opening of the Mohawk Trail in 1920, North Adams erected a sign, "This is the City of North Adams, the Mother of the Mohawk Trail." Indignant Adams put up its own sign at the boundary: "You are now leaving Adams, the Mother of North Adams and the Grandmother of the Mohawk Trail." (AAS)

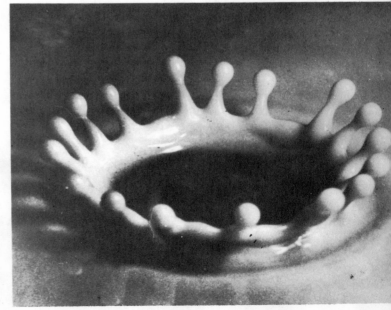

ONE DROP OF MILK in a saucer, caught at its maximum burst, was photographed for the first time and reproduced around the world. The technical triumph was made possible by a revolutionary ultra-rapid or stroboscopic camera, developed at the Massachusetts Institute of Technology in Cambridge by Prof. Harold Edgerton. The stroboscopic light, developed in the 1920s, allowed even bullets to be viewed when stopped in mid-flight. The rapid light blink became a basic tool of industry, and mini-strobes now pop brightly wherever cameras are used. (MIT)

THE CITY ROOM of the *Boston Post*, once the largest morning newspaper in America with a circulation of 450,000, as it appeared in full clutter in 1923. The *Post* expired on October 4, 1956. Note on the desk at right the pile of city directories—the bible of newspapers.

"THOUGH THE TOMB IS SEALED, the dry bones still rattle," wrote columnist Heywood Broun of the Sacco and Vanzetti case which was tried in Dedham's granite courthouse in 1921—and around the world. It began on April 15, 1920, when a shoe company's paymaster in South Braintree and his guard were killed by two men who escaped with over $15,000. Because they somewhat resembled descriptions by witnesses, Sacco and Vanzetti were charged with the crime. Both carried firearms, were anarchists, had evaded the army draft, and had made false statements upon arrest. They were also in fear of deportation. Anti-foreign sentiment was sweeping the nation, and the death sentence was thought to be a result of it. Brilliant lawyers fought the case on both sides, using the headlines as dueling swords. An appeal for retrial was denied in 1927 by the Massachusetts supreme judicial court. Protest meetings were held, appeals made to Gov. Alvan T. Fuller, who appointed an advisory committee and found that the judicial procedures had been legal. Sacco and Vanzetti were executed on August 22, 1927, to the accompaniment of world-wide demonstrations of sympathy and protest. Much of the evidence has been discredited, but new tests with sophisticated ballistics equipment seemed to prove that Sacco's gun had killed the guard. The case still has not been fully resolved. In July 1977, though, a judge concluded that there had not been enough evidence in the case—posthumously exonerating Sacco and Vanzetti. In the photograph, Sacco is at right. (WT&G)

BUSY INSPECTORS are buying Spanish grapes at wholesale in a warehouse in Charlestown about 1925. The elegant purchaser wearing the Chesterfield with velvet collar (center right) probably represents one of the more fastidious purveyors, S. S. Pierce & Co., which catered to the Boston Brahmins.

FISHERMAN'S MEMORIAL, one of a number of famous art works in Massachusetts, confronts the sea at Gloucester bearing the biblical theme "They that go down to the sea in ships that do business in great waters." The statue by local sculptor Leonard Craske was chosen during Gloucester's tercentenary in 1923 and dedicated to its fishermen on August 23, 1925. Total cost of the memorial was about $20,000. Craske, who died at seventy-three, and once slept in Central Park during his struggling years, said: "The greatest discovery I've made since the advent of the Depression is that anybody can do without a statue."

THEY THAT GO
DOWN TO THE SEA
IN SHIPS
1623 — 1923

FOUR PRESIDENTS came from Massachusetts—a record number for any state. The unlikely cowboy at a July 4th celebration in 1927 at Rapid City, South Dakota, is Calvin Coolidge, 30th president of the United States, who won the popular name of "Silent Cal." Mrs. Coolidge is seated on the grass. President from 1923 to 1929, he was catapulted into national fame—and the presidency—by using Massachusetts militia to end a police strike in Boston in 1919. Other presidents from Massachusetts were John Adams, John Quincy Adams, and John F. Kennedy. (WT&G)

THE GREAT PONZI at the height of his flim-flam in Boston in the 1930s: This dapper, nervous bantam became a translating clerk for an import-export firm and a wizard at manipulating other people's money by robbing Peter to pay Paul. In eight months, he manipulated millions before the FBI put him in the pen and deported him to Italy in 1934. He died a pauper in Rio de Janeiro in 1949. (Boston University)

A SIXTY-POUND TURKEY is hard to find, but one was raised in South Royalston in the early 1940s by Henry L. Sargent, a tool grinder, who won the bird in an American Legion raffle. "The bird was all skin and bone when I got him," Sargent said at the time, "Everyone said I got stuck. I fed him plain oats right out of the bag. Took a quart to a feed—just like a hog." When Sargent was at work, his mother took care of the turkey, and she said: "He eats all the time. Sometimes he'll eat three quarts a day. That's enough for a horse. I keep food by him all the time." The broad-breasted bronze, never bred, developed a nasty temper and had to be tied by clothes line to a stake. He was given the name of Billy the Great, and when he puffed up, the enormity and energy of him was frightening, creating a storm of dust around flailing wings, scarlet head, and puffed wattles. In about 1947 when Billy began to lose weight, the owner gave him to Baldwinville Hospital Cottages for Children, a home for the crippled. "He was shown around three times before they cooked him," Sargent related. "They got three meals on it and even made soup of the bones."

[83]

A GLOUCESTER TRAWLER unloads a fat catch of cod—the traditional fish of Massachusetts—into new barrels. The most frequent procedure in Gloucester when huge shipments come in is to set up conveyor belts that will carry the cargo directly to the filleting and quick-freeze plants, one of which can be glimpsed across the water at right. (MDC&D)

A DEPOSED ROYAL FAMILY, the Empress Zita (dressed in mourning) and the royal family of Austria pose on a hot afternoon on August 29, 1944, in the small town of Royalston. They had come from Quebec to vacation at the summer home of Mrs. Calvin Bullock, widow of a wealthy New York stockbroker whom they visited regularly for several years. From left to right are the Archduke Charles, the Archduchess Elizabeth, the Archduchess Adelhaid, Archduke Felix, Archduchess Charlotte, and Archduke Otto, who would have been king.

WORLD WAR II pushed another royal family into exile, this time from Holland to Lee, Massachusetts, where they spent the summer of 1942. Queen Wilhelmina of Holland is at right. Her daughter, Princess Juliana, is accompanied by her two children, Irene and Beatrix as they arrive in the area. (Rex Fall)

THE BIGGEST ROBBERY in the nation took place in Boston on January 17, 1950, when eight men held up a Brink's money transfer and escaped with $2,775,395.12 of which $1,218,211.20 was cash. Only about $50,000 was recovered. The thieves were caught, tried, and convicted. They are seen here at the start of the fifth day of their trial on August 10, 1956 in Superior Court. From left: Anthony Pino, 49; James I. Faherty, 45; Henry Baker, 50; Adolph Maffie, 45; Thomas F. Richardson, 49; Michael V. Geagan, 47; Vincent J. Costa, 42; Joseph F. McGinnis, 52; and Paul Smith, chief defense counsel. (WT&G)

LAW AND ORDER by Massachusetts State Police puts the sledgehammer to a group of confiscated slot machines, or one-arm bandits as the newspapers delighted in calling them. The cherries will never whirl again on these—but others were being manufactured at this very moment in the late 1940s. (WT&G)

MEMBERS OF THE MEDIA witness *Mayflower II* as she glides into Plymouth Harbor in 1957. The ship was built in England from the original drawings and as far as humanly possible stuck to the ribs of the original. The full-scale reproduction is berthed at State pier in Plymouth.

THE BIRTH CONTROL PILL, which has affected the world's population and the women's liberation movement, began here in 1956 at the Worcester Foundation for Experimental Biology. Co-developers were Dr. Gregory Pincus (seated), Dr. John Rock, and Dr. Celso Ramon Garcia (left). A fourth, Dr. Min Chueh Chang, is absent. (Marvin Richmond, Worcester)

Hermits and Midgets

MASSACHUSETTS had a number of male hermits who eschewed humanity and crept off into woods to nurse their hurts for whatever reasons. Some had been spurned by women and never got over it. Others, racked by war wounds, sought the balm of isolation. They lived in the crude shelter of caves once frequented by bears and Indians. or built crude shacks of driftwood and logs cut from their clearing.

Victims of unrequited love drew the most visitors, usually women who came bearing straw baskets of nourishment. For such treats the hermits occasionally bathed, cut their whiskers, and combed their hair, but not too often. They must have had female counterparts, but these have remained anonymous in the back rooms of family homes perhaps, preferring less of isolation to more of civilization's protection and comfort.

Authentic hermits were pack rats who kept scrounged twigs in brown paper bags tied with string. They also fed neighborhood wild animals, such as raccoons, chipmunks, and squirrels. Some were hard-working, some were just downright cantankerous, but all were so sensitive to the abrasiveness of society that seldom, if ever, did they return to it.

The opposite was true of the life style of Massachusetts' midgets. Some were well enough known and in the public eye so much that they made a niche in history. P. T. Barnum brought a group of miniatures together that reached international fame, just as did many of his ingenious attractions. He became the world's most renowned showman, even taking his midgets to London to charm Queen Victoria.

[87]

A HERMIT OF NANTUCKET, otherwise unidentified, amid the clutter and flotsam he had collected. (AAS)

HIDDEN IN THE WOODS of Worcester in a section once called Rattlesnake Hill is a phenomenal act of dedication known as the "Deed On the Rock." In 219 words, all in capital letters about an inch and a half high, is a legal document chiseled out of a smooth, gray fieldstone ledge: ". . . I do hereby acknowledge, do hereby grant, sell and convey unto God . . . this land, to be governed by the above mentioned laws and together with the Spirit of God," part of it reads. The deed was the work of Solomon Parsons, a labor of love that took years. Parsons, who lost his son in the Civil War and was a farmer and a vegetarian for fifty years, built a primitive temple 100 yards from his rocky deed and conducted services there for thirty to forty each Sunday. He died at ninety-three on December 16, 1893.

A HERMIT OF QUIDNET, a Nantucket fishing village, photographed about 1870. (AAS)

HIS TERRACED PLOT on Prospect Hill near Waltham shows that this hermit was hard-working—an unusual trait, for many were misanthropists involved in self-pity. (AAS)

HERMIT BILL and his hermitage in Barre about the turn of the century: For this special occasion, the hermit had his hair cut and his beard trimmed, probably at the request of the photographer, who paid for it. (AAS)

ANOTHER HERMIT, unidentified, deep in the woods with his rifle at his left: His home is an authentic hermitage, filled with determination and amateur hammering. (AAS)

THE FAMOUS HERMIT of Erving Castle: In an 1877 Massachusetts gazette, Rev. Elias Nason, describing the farming town of Erving wrote: "In a secluded ledge which rises almost perpendicularly, far up on the right bank of the [Miller's] river, there now lives a hermit, bearing the name of 'John Smith,' who calls his rocky habitation 'The Erving Castle.' He is a man of some intelligence, wears a long beard and Scotch cap, and receives his visitors with a kindly spirit. He spends his time in knitting stockings, picking berries, cutting wood, reading and writing, and entertaining company. His age may be fifty years, three of which he has spent in 'Erving Castle.'" John Smith also found time to collaborate on two autobiographies, which he sold. The 1868 version tells that he was a dry-goods pedlar in the Scottish Highlands, where he met a girl of "rare beauty, pleasing manner and queenly bearing." Too shy to reveal his feelings and believing his station in life too low, he failed to make his feelings known. Meanwhile the beauty eloped to England with a cattle dealer. "Before this disappointment," John Smith wrote, "I was enterprising, ambitious, doing well at my business and cherishing bright dreams of the future." The 1871 version is different. John was on stage as an actor in a passionate love scene. His beloved in the audience walked out—the unpardonable sin. In any event, the professional hermit attracted many visitors, especially women bearing gifts. (AAS)

[91]

THE APPEALING MIDGET leaning on her cane in this rare photograph is Dolly Dutton, born Alice M. Dutton in Natick in 1855 of normal-sized parents. Weighing two and a half pounds at birth, she was small enough to fit into a sugar bowl, according to family legend. At eighteen, she only weighed twelve pounds and at twenty-seven, stood three feet high. She joined the Barnum troupe and was known as the Lilliputian of America and the Little Fairy. When twenty, she was married to B. F. Sawin, also a member of the troupe, and described as a Lilliputian pepper-pod. He lost interest in marriage after a few months and abused her. An only child died in infancy. Dolly Dutton became schizophrenic, and at twenty-seven was committed to the State Lunatic Hospital in Worcester, where she died of epilepsy on January 6, 1890. On stage, one of her recitations was "The Little Maid." The last stanza went: "Now all ye little maids/ A moral I will give you/Don't trust to little men/They surely will deceive you." (Lydia Eva Dutton Merrils)

WHEN THE MOST FAMOUS MIDGET of them all, Gen. Tom Thumb (Charles S. Stratton) died in 1883, he left his widow, the former Mercy Lavinia Bump Warren. She was born in Middleboro of normal-sized parents. At ten she reached her full growth of thirty-nine inches. In the Barnum troupe of miniatures with Lavinia and the general were two Bolognese midgets—Count Primo Magri and his brother, Baron Ernest Magri. Rumors had been afloat for some time when Lavinia made this statement: "My intended husband is Count Primo Magri, between 35 and 36, a member of a distinguished Italian family; a count in his own right, master of several languages, and accomplished scholar, a finished and dexterous swordsman and a perfect gentleman. We are not to be married in a dime museum, nor with fireworks and a brass band. . . . our union will be the result of mutual respect and admiration between a gentleman, who, though small of stature, is every inch a man, and a lady who fancies that the public should by this time know her to be a woman of sense." Show business proved to be too arduous and the couple retired to Lavinia's family home in Middleboro where they built a refreshment stand next door called "Primo's Pastime." Lavinia died on November 25, 1919, at seventy-eight, and is buried beside her first husband in Bridgeport, Connecticut, under a small stone reading, "His Wife." A forty-foot shaft of Italian marble, topped with a life-size figure, honors Tom Thumb. The Count, who dreamed warm dreams of his native land and decided to return, held an auction to dispose of everything, but died before he could begin the journey.

COUNT AND COUNTESS Primo Magri of Middleboro in a rare photograph taken in front of their refreshment stand, "Primo's Pastime." (MHA)

Notable Massachusetts Characters

AMONG NOTABLE CHARACTERS in Massachusetts, or any other place, can be included the distinguished, the accomplished, the inimitable, the notorious, the fashionable, even the peculiar—those that in one way or another are worthy of our admiration or our wonderment. One or two might be added for the sake of humor.

The earliest "character" recorded in Massachusetts was in 1625, when Thomas Morton of Merry Mount set up shop with the Indians in Wollaston, later Quincy. A wealthy man, author of two books, sharp-tongued, independent, and free-living, Morton found the Massachusetts Bay Colony to be situated in a paradise. "If this land be not rich, then is the whole world poore," he wrote. Among other phenomena he noted was that five hundred to one thousand lobsters beat in with each tide. For five years he used them only for bait.

Rivalry in fur trading and religious prejudice (Morton was an Anglican and an epitome of the anti-Puritan) led to bitter enmity with the Plymouth settlers. What raised their ruff particularly were certain festivities at Merry Mount around a Maypole, involving local Indians and the use of strong spirits. Morton was arrested three times, sent to England for trial, but managed to return each time. On his last trip he was imprisoned in Boston for nearly a year and later moved to Maine, where he died. Merry Mount lives on in the official seal of Quincy.

FOR JOHN FOSTER BY JOHN FOSTER—and probably his masterpiece: Although only thirty-three when he died, Foster achieved a full and remarkable life. He was Boston's first printer, compiled one of the early almanacs, wrote a book about comets, and engraved the seal of Massachusetts. His stone-cutting career extended from 1653 to 1695, with examples starkly standing in nearly all the old burial grounds in and near Boston. When news of his impending death reached Increase Mather, he sent a Latin verse: "Living thou studiest the stars; dying, mayst thou Foster, I pray, mount above the skies and learn to measure the highest heaven." Replied Foster: "I measure it and it is mine; the Lord has bought it for me; nor am I held to pay aught for it but thanks." The couplets are on the tombstone in Dorchester with author credits, I. M. and J. F. (Daniel Farber, Worcester)

PHILLIS WHEATLEY, first black American writer and author of a book of poetry published in England: She attracted considerable attention and favor, including honors in England and a meeting with George Washington after writing a poem in his honor. Brought from Africa—possibly Senegal—as a slave in 1760 about age seven, she remembered little of her previous life except that her mother poured out water as a libation to the rising sun. John Wheatley, a cultivated Boston tailor, bought her to attend his wife, Susannah. Within sixteen months, Phillis was able to read fluently the most difficult parts of the Bible. She was given every educational opportunity and liberty, and encouraged to write poetry. Uncertain health, the death of her benefactors, marriage to John Peters—who failed as baker, grocer, doctor, and lawyer—and the death of two children, brought her own death at only thirty-one on December 5, 1784. Her last child died in time to be buried in the same unmarked grave.

A HORSE-DRAWN procession of carriages and heavily loaded wagons en route from Leicester, Massachusetts, to Newport, Rhode Island, paused on a hot day in 1777 at the edge of Scott's Pond while the driver of the lead sulky clucked his horse to water. Stung by an insect, the horse bolted, drowning the driver, Aaron Lopez, before the eyes of his frantic wife and children riding behind him. So ended the career of an unusual man whom Dr. Ezra Stiles, president of Yale College, called "a Merchant of the first Eminence; for Honor & Extent of Commerce probably surpassed by no Mercht in America." At his peak, Lopez was owner, or part-owner, of 113 ships in world trade. He had married twice, fathering seven children by his first wife, Abigail, who died, and ten by his second, Sarah. Siding with the American cause in the Revolution, Lopez took his colony of about seventy Newport Jews ahead of British capture and sacking of the town, and moved to the small inland Massachusetts town of Leicester, where he opened a "noted place for trade." After the war, the colony returned to Newport. War and inflation pushed the Lopez estate of $100,000 into bankruptcy, but a son, Joseph, paid all debts. One haunting directive sent by Lopez to his captains everywhere was that should any Jew in peril seek safety, he was to be taken to a safe harbor. (WT&G)

THE ARISTOCRATIC FACE of Charles Bulfinch in 1786 at twenty-three, as painted by Mather Brown: The famous American architect, born in Boston, put his personal stamp on many important structures, including the Capitol in Washington, Boston's state house, University Hall at Harvard University, and Massachusetts General Hospital. He designed the Federal Street Theatre in Boston, the first theater in New England, no longer standing.

"LORD" TIMOTHY DEXTER *(right)* remains in Massachusetts history as one of the more famous eccentrics. For company, he hired a ship-carver to execute forty, eight-foot statues of famous men, mounted about his green-shuttered, white mansion in a "harlequinade in wood." Vulgar and ignorant, Dexter lived among sycophants and parasites who fed his egomania. A tanner by trade, he saw easier ways and made a fortune by buying depreciated Continental currency and by sharp mercantile trading. He gave himself his title, along with an inscription on one of two statues of himself on his property: "I am first in the East, the first in the West and the Greatest Philosopher in the known world." A fish pedlar with a similar turn of mind became Lord Dexter's personal poet laureate and proclaimed: "Lord Dexter is a man of fame,/ Most celebrated is his name,/ More precious far than gold that's pure,/ Lord Dexter shines forever more!" Dexter staged his own funeral, watched the scene from an upstairs room, and before it ended was beating his wife for not weeping. He was a favorite client of a local oracle, Madam Hooper, a former teacher turned fortune teller, and in 1802 wrote a book, *A Pickle for the Knowing Ones,* an autobiography. The work had his own spelling and no punctuation. This was remedied in a second edition where he inserted a page of "stops" so that readers could "peper and salt it as they please." Lord Dexter died October 26, 1806, but reserved a place in history.

AN EARLY WORCESTER BEAUTY, Mrs. J. Henry Hill, in an ambrotype—a nineteenth-century reproduction process in which a glass slide of thin density appeared as a positive when put against a dark background. (AAS)

A MIGHTY HUNTER who tamed grizzly bears was John "Grizzly" Adams, shown in a rare photograph. He is wearing his fringed buckskin suit and cap made of a wolf's head trimmed with tails. Believed to have been born in Medway on October 20, 1807, Adams was a cobbler's apprentice who learned how to live off the land in what were the wilds of New England in the 1820s. Later, staked by a brother who had hit it rich in the California gold diggings, Adams began collecting and taming grizzlies and wrote a book that made him famous. "Once, annoyed by a barking and howling coyote," he related, "I drew my revolver and cried: 'Die, base beast, unworthy the boon of life; take the reward of your audacity,' A shot felled him; when, placing my foot upon his neck and plunging my knife through his heart, I exclaimed, 'Die, coward of the wilderness!' and kicked the body from me." He bore other names: James Capen Adams, James C. Adams, the Great Hunter, Gray Beard, Old Adams, Grizzly Adams, *Hyas Tyes* (Great Chief), The Wild Yankee, and Old Grizzly Adams. In April 1860, he joined Barnum for a brief but successful tour, then took to his bed after one of his grizzlies, General Fremont, had laid open his head for the third or fourth time. "I'm a used-up man," said Adams before he died in Neponset.

EXOTIC, ROMANTIC TALES are plentiful in yesterday's Massachusetts, and one of the classics is surely that of Madame Jumel, who once lived in a dugout under a Massachusetts hill as a child. Born at sea in 1767 as Elizabeth Brown, or Bowen, she was placed in a Providence workhouse for three years, while her sister, Polly, her mother, Phoebe, and her stepfather, Jonathan Clark, lived precariously as public charges, warned out of Providence, Rehoboth, Taunton, and North Brookfield. As an extremely attractive woman, Betsy later, while in Paris, took the eye of a wealthy wine merchant, Stephen Jumel. She married him and returned to New York to live in his elegant mansion, bought in 1810, that housed her Paris wardrobe and a notable collection of art and furniture. The shabby little workhouse girl had come a long way. After Jumel died in 1832, she was married in 1833 to Aaron Burr, then eighty years old, but divorced him after a year. She died in 1865. Betsy's home became the Jumel Mansion, a showpiece of history.

THE POET Henry Wadsworth Longfellow and his second wife out for a walk pause before Craigie House, their magnificent mansion on Brattle Street in Cambridge. The house still stands as a National Historic Site. It became Washington's headquarters on July 2, 1775. Longfellow bought it in 1843, along with eight acres of the original two hundred that went with it, and according to an account of the day, "keeps up the ancient renown of the house as to style and hospitality." (AAS)

THE MAN FROM WALDEN—Henry David Thoreau, in one of three Maxham daguerreotype portraits of him: Surely the most notable Massachusetts hermit of all, Thoreau was a Yankee as well as a transcendentalist, but his practical teaching was not that everyone should live alone in the woods but that each man should be true to his inner self regardless of the pressures of society. Walden Pond and Thoreau's home are today a state reservation which attracts many visitors annually.

[97]

JOHN GREENLEAF WHITTIER (1807-1892), born near Haverhill, became one of the nation's best-known poets and the voice of New England before the Industrial Revolution. A pioneer in regional literature, he was also a crusader for humanitarian causes and a reformer. Forgotten in time is that he was a founder of the Republican Party. Among his memorable poems was "Snow-Bound," never surpassed in its mood; "Maud Muller"; "Barbara Frietchie"; "The Barefoot Boy"; and many others. His eloquent voice was best heard in his native role as a Massachusetts villager. (NYPL)

JULIA WARD HOWE (1819-1910), author of "The Battle Hymn of the Republic," was also a fervent abolitionist, reformer, and writer who loved to have her picture taken. Born Julia Ward, daughter of a banker, she married Samuel Gridley Howe, a Boston reformer and teacher of the blind. The economic hardships of Civil War widows stirred her to work for more equal education and economic opportunities for women, and to found women's clubs and equal suffrage groups. She is best remembered for "The Battle Hymn of the Republic," one of the most stirring war hymns ever written, which was first published in the *Atlantic Monthly* in February 1862. She poses here in a favorite basket chair. (NYPL)

THE PATRIOT FERVOR of the Civil War is apparent in Worcester at the dedication of a tombstone to a Massachusetts hero, Brig. Gen. George H. Ward. A descendant of Gen. Artemas Ward who preceded Washington as the commanding officer of Revolutionary forces, Ward led the 15th Regiment, Massachusetts Volunteers, in some of the bloodiest battles of the Civil War. In the disastrous battle of Ball's Bluff in October 1861, he was wounded and underwent amputation below one knee. He rejoined his regiment and, at Gettysburg, he took a miniball in the thigh which severed a femoral artery, causing his death on July 4, 1863. The regiment lost over half its officers and men in the Battle of the Wilderness. (WHS)

[98]

"IT WAS CONFESSEDLY the most distinguished affair that ever occurred in Lowell," wrote the *Lowell Weekly Journal,* of a wedding on July 21, 1870. The principals were Miss Blanche Butler—daughter of a congressman, Gen. Benjamin Franklin Butler—and Maj. Gen. Adelbert Ames, a senator from Mississippi. The scene is on the portico of the Butler's Regency-style mansion in Lowell, and the bride, displaying her gown, is surrounded by the formal wedding party. "This was one of the most elegant dresses that could be worn on such an occasion," rhapsodized *The Boston Post*. General Butler was one of the most hated Union officers in the Civil War, with his portrait painted at the bottom of chamber pots and a broadside from Confederates proclaiming him a felon to be hanged if captured. At the time of his daughter's marriage, Butler was a rabid radical Republican and one of the House managers who conducted impeachment proceedings against Pres. Andrew Johnson. (AAS)

APPLE MARY, one of the familiar Boston sights on the Common in the 1880s, was also known as the Apple Woman. Her stand was near one of the great trees close by the Park Square entrance.

A CRIMEAN WAR VETERAN, playing an organette and bearing notice of his permit, No. 15, collects coins in his fur-lined hat on Front Street, Worcester, about 1870.

WITH NINETEENTH-CENTURY SURREALISM, multi-millionaire William Emerson Baker of Wellesley, presides at a general invitation to his tenth anniversary at Ridge Hill Farms. Baker was noted for his sumptuous fetes, full of surprises for his guests. An elaborate formal garden held secret passageways, trap doors, pillars, archways, and grotesque faces. The Den of Fancies and Frivolities was a rocky strip of land along a $50,000 artificial lake, where trees had been trained into fantastic forms, clothed, or painted so as to represent men and animals in ridiculous positions. In one place was a whiskey bottle ten feet high, made of beer bottles strung upon wires and pipes. It was labeled: "The Last of the Spirits." As a visitor crossed a dark chasm on a narrow bridge, a savage-looking black with a club brandished over his head would leap out from behind a rock—activated by a secret spring in the flooring. Not far away was a bench and a sign in front of a cactus plant: "The demoniacal cereus blooms every ten minutes on sunny days." The visitor would sit to wait; then the bench would collapse, and a red devil would rise from the earth with the cactus upon his head. "Mr. Baker's ambition seems to have been to make people laugh, and he has succeeded," reported a newspaper of the day. He died in 1888 at fifty-nine. (AAS)

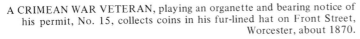

A RELAXING GROUP of reporters allow themselves to be captured on a glass plate during the 1875 Regimental Reunion of the GAR at Salem Neck. The front-seat syndrome which comes from being the "mirror of the truth" is much in evidence. (AAS)

THE WELL-DRESSED WIFE of a prominent Worcester banker, Mrs. Daniel Waldo, Jr., in the fashion of her day: The photograph was made from an oil painting done in the early 1800s. (AAS)

THESE TAUNTON CITIZENS, the L. B. Jackson family, impressed the photographer so much around 1880 that he made a stereoscopic view of them. (AAS)

QUIETLY BRILLIANT in their innovative way, the Shaker brethren of Hancock, shown here with their dairy herd in 1885, built this great circular barn of stone in 1826. The town had more than its share of stone—it was originally called Jericho from the high walls or mountains on each side. The unusual barn was 270 feet in circumference, with walls laid in lime for which the masons were paid 500 dollars and boarded. "The mast and rafters are 53 feet in length and united at the top," revealed an early account. "On the lower floor are stables 8 feet high, including the manger, which is inward, and into which convenient places are left for throwing hay and feed from above. A span of horses and 52 horned cattle may be stabled. The covering of the stables forms the barn floor on to which from an offset there is but one large doorway for teams, which make the circuit of the floor, and pass out at the same place. Eight or ten can occupy the floor at the same time; the hay is thrown into the large area in the center." (Amy Bess Miller, Pittsfield)

A ROUND DANCE, from an old engraving, shows a Shaker community in four circles of dancers surrounding a group of singers at the center. More correctly called the American branch of the United Society of Believers in Christ's Second Appearing, the sect received its name because of the rhythmic movement, or shaking, that was an essential part of its ceremonies. Massachusetts had at least five settlements, the first two founded by "Mother Ann" Lee, an English religious visionary who, although illiterate, claimed the gift of tongues, the ability to work miracles, and the sense of when spirits were present. (Hancock Shaker Village)

[102]

THE SHAKERS, who have died out as a result of their celibacy, had several types of ritual dances, another version of which is shown here. Rhythmic movement, they believed, would shake off their sins.

A CURIOUS JOURNEY forgotten in time was accomplished in June 1882 by sixty-two-year old Civil War pensioner Warren B. Johnson of Webster. While in California to recover his health, Johnson became homesick and decided to return by wagon, accompanied by his horse, Fanny; a cow, Bessie; and a dog, Bert. The unusual trip of more than forty-five hundred miles took nearly two years, but he finally arrived, wet his feet in the Atlantic, and wrote a book in 1887 entitled *From the Pacific to the Atlantic: Being an Account of a Journey Overland from Eureka, Humboldt Co., California, to Webster, Worcester Co., Mass., with a Horse, Carriage, Cow and Dog.* As he approached Webster, an escort of carriages and a crowd on foot led him into town. This illustration was made shortly after his arrival.

FIRST WOMAN OF AMERICAN LETTERS, Edith Wharton, as she was photographed in 1905. Three years before, she had moved into her new home on 128 acres in Lenox, where she lived until 1910.

BLACK WORLD-CHAMPION bicycle rider and gold-medal winner at twenty was the impressive record of Marshall W. "Major" Taylor of Worcester who won the one-mile event at the 1899 International Meet in Montreal, considered the highest honor in the cycling world. He went on during the same day to win a second victory in the two-mile open event. Taylor's remarkable career was made even more memorable because of the racial prejudice that pursued him in most of his meets.

AT ATTENTION is World War I hero Lt. Col. Charles W. Whittlesey of Pittsfield as he receives the Congressional Medal of Honor on Boston Common for his heroic action in the Argonne as leader of the Lost Battalion, whose exploits had thrilled patriotic America. After launching an attack early in October 1918, about six hundred men under then-Major Whittlesey, were cut off by German forces and put up a heroic defense for five days without food, water, or reserve ammunition, refusing surrender despite several heavy barrages and attacks. Some four hundred of them were killed before rescue came from American relief troops. Affixing the medal is Maj. Gen. Clarence R. Edwards.

THE SPACE AGE BEGAN HERE on the afternoon of March 16, 1926, when physicist Dr. Robert H. Goddard of Worcester sent his first liquid-fuel rocket soaring from the meadow of his Great-Aunt Effy Ward's farm on Pakachoag Hill, Auburn. The soar was forty-one feet. Newspaper headlines were waggish about what seemed like a mad professor's dream to reach the moon, but Goddard's faith was constant. From that cold, overcast winter day on the hill, mankind's vista of knowledge was to increase by billions of miles. Goddard posed for this picture just before contact and ignition of the rocket by means of a blowtorch. The crude pioneer rocket is now in the Smithsonian. (WT&G)

THE MISSING LETTER "D" alters the whole picture. George H. "Ducky" Jordan *(inset),* a rural mail carrier of Grafton, began selling Fords in 1913, qualifying for a huge illuminated sign as the largest local dealer. Jordan remembered the Model-T as "wonderful, but people were not ready yet for a fast car." And there were arguments about "piston slap." He threatened to give up the agency; Detroit couldn't believe it. "If you don't think I'm going, just count the days I'm gone," said Jordan. The Ford Company insisted he remove the sign. Jordan said he would—for $1,500. Ford countered with $500, then a law suit—and photographers to take pictures. Before they came, Jordan slipped out and pried the big D out of the sign. The photographers did their work the next morning. Jordan said that Henry Ford fired them all and did nothing more. "The sign is a kind of landmark. People stop in to ask about it. I keep it painted regular." The sharp-tongued independent Yankee died in 1958 at the age of seventy. (WT&G)

THE LAST PUBLIC APPEARANCE of Henry Beston, author of the nature classic *The Outermost House,* was at Eastham, Cape Cod, during national literary memorial ceremonies marking the site where he wrote his book. On the chill October day, Mrs. Beston, a noted author in her own right, enjoys a blanket over her feet from Mrs. Endicott Peabody, the wife of the governor of Massachusetts. Henry Beston spent a year writing his book of man and the earth, and the four seasons, a classic about famous Cape Cod, with soaring prose and fundamental truths. "Do no dishonour to the earth lest you dishonour the spirit of man," he wrote in his final paragraph. "Touch the earth, love the earth, honour the earth, her plains, her valleys, her hills, and her seas; rest your spirit in her solitary places. For the gifts of life are the earth's and they are given to all." (Toni Peabody)

A FORGOTTEN MOMENT in the passing scene took place on November 25, 1946, at 5:45 p.m. in Worcester at the corner of Main and Austin streets, when a stubborn unidentified woman and an obstinate bus driver clashed. This photo was published in nearly every major newspaper in the United States and in a number of national magazines. Radio commentators over national hookups discussed the story and sought her name in vain. *Life* devoted a full page to the photograph. *Time* named her as Woman of the Year, and wrote: "She learned (what she had long suspected) that privation marched with the victorious armies as well as with the vanquished. Her frustration was sharply symbolized by one elderly woman of Worcester, Mass., who stood on a street corner futilely waving while bus after crowded bus passed her by. Finally she stamped her foot and for 20 minutes she and the driver fought a duel of wills, as obdurate as two peace-making statesmen. This unidentified Worcesterite, impatient at the complexities that lay between her and simple goals, was the Woman of the Year." A *Worcester Telegram* reporter, with the promise of three days off if he found her, did. She was Mrs. Cora D. O'Connor, forty-two, mother of three. "I'm the one," she said. "I've been ashamed of it ever since." Her husband was on the same bus. (Edward Cournoyer, Worcester-WT&G)

Natural Happenings

IT ALMOST SEEMED as if nature had given every Massachusetts city and town a plaything singularly its own—a natural landmark that could be stared at again and again, and shown to visiting relatives and friends. Most of the time, it was made of rock, of which the state has a plenitude. The singular rocks were all given names, depending on their resemblance to frog, whale, pulpit, egg, or even the Devil.

Many still may be seen. The Puritan heritage kept the satanic theme alive with Devil's Bed and Pillow, on a tiny island of No Man's Land eight miles off West Tisbury in Martha's Vineyard; the Devil's Pulpit, a strange, white marble formation jutting from the sheer-summit cliff of Monument Mountain south of Stockbridge; and the Devil's Football, a magnetic boulder of 300 tons in South Hadley. Legend holds that Satan kicked it from Devil's Garden at Amherst Notch several miles distant.

There is more to nature's works in Massachusetts, however, than its providing each locale with a favorite landmark. The weather, in the summer deliciously refreshing and inviting, in winter takes on the stern, forbidding face that is so well respected in the northern states. Snow and gales, ice and sleet, rain and floods were regular occurrences yesterday, just as they are now. And added to all of these grim visitations were the disasters caused by fire, which were much more feared in the past than they are today because of methods and materials used for building construction, the lack of sophisticated fire-fighting equipment, and the fireplace and coal stove.

As an example of one of nature's pranks from earlier days, the Great Snowstorm of 1717 was never equalled, at least in Middleboro. An account of it was kept by descendants of the Morton family and reprinted in *The Middleborough Antiquarian:*

The storm commenced on Sunday and lasted till Wednesday night. The snow descended to the depth of seven feet and often, when drifted, to the depth of ten or twelve. The windows of all the lower stories were darkened, making the house look gloomy and tomb-like within. So great was the weights of the snow on the roof, that the inhabitants feared that it would be crushed in, and they carried up supporters into the garret, to prevent it. They dug paths under the snow to the barn, and packed the snow, taken out, into the leanto in the rear of the house. They could get no water to drink, (the well being some distance from the house,) and they had to melt snow for their own use, and that of their cattle. They saw none of their neighbors, at the old Morton house, for three days. Then Mr. Abraham Miller, their nearest neighbor, came walking over the snow on snow-shoes. He said, "I walked over the top of my own orchard, coming here, and I could see only the tops of many of the trees. I should have thought that I had been walking through a field filled with bushes, instead of apple-trees. I could not make myself believe that it was my own orchard I was walking over." He had come to borrow meal for his family use, as it was impossible to mill through the deep snows, and the families in the neighborhood had to depend on each other for meal until they could break their way to the mill. After the snows, came a thaw and a freshet, owing to the rapid melting of the great body of snow that lay on the ground. The Nemasket river presented a roaring flood, overflowing its banks and endangering all the houses that stood near its shores, and tearing away the foundations of both bridges and gristmills, by its furious current. It was such a freshet as had never before been seen, and the great snow-storm and the freshet that followed were never forgotten during the life time of the old inhabitants of the town of Middleboro.

DEVIL'S PULPIT on the May farm in the southwestern part of Leominster. (AAS)

PUBLIC COLD WATER: This drinking fountain in Gilbertville maintained by the Women's Christian Temperance Union was an aid to the strength and resolution of men and agile boys who were encouraged to quaff its pure waters. (AAS)

Rollstone Boulder, Fitchburg, Mass.

ROLLSTONE BOULDER in Fitchburg on its original site on Rollstone Hill: By intent, the man in this view looks as if he is carrying a giant sandwich. In a sentimental gesture the city later had the rock split along natural clefts and resettled in the midst of Main Street where everyone could see it. (AAS)

THE BALANCED ROCK in Pittsfield is plentiful with graffiti, including a tribute to Pres. William McKinley, who died September 14, 1901, from an assassin's bullet.

ROCKING STONE, beside a fashionable demonstrator, chaperone, and dog in the town of Barre: The natural curiosity is actually two rocks. In fact, explained an early account, "The lower one rests on a ledge some 20 feet high and is itself about 10 to 12 feet in altitude. On top of it rests another boulder eight feet high. These make it look as though the first high wind would send them tumbling over the ledge and yet they have stood there for ages." (AAS)

BALANCE ROCK in Lanesboro, a 165-ton, triangular-shaped, limestone boulder, rests three feet above ground on another rock in such a manner that it vibrates when touched. Geologists reveal that it was carried by glacial action to the Pittsfield area from some point east of the Hudson River. (MDC&D)

Old Bull Frog Rock near New Boston

OLD BULLFROG ROCK squatted mightily near the village of New Boston in the western Massachusetts town of Sandisfield. (AAS)

THE INTRIGUING, UNFINISHED EFFECT of Profile Rock on Joshua's Mountain, Taunton, made it a favorite with picnickers and photographers. (AAS)

THE PROFILE, an outcropping of rock near Stockbridge, was another competitor of New Hampshire's famous Old Man of the Mountain. (AAS)

CROSS ROCK, in an open field in Pittsfield: The plenitude of rocks indicates the problems of early farmers and the reason Massachusetts has so many stone walls. (AAS)

UNGEON ROCK in the western part of ynn, two miles from the city, was more dely known than most natural phenoma. It was supposed to have been a hide-it for a band of pirates under the leadership of Claudius Morillo, who stored treasure there. The earthquake of 1658 aled the cave, turning it into a dungeon.

On June 5, 1851, Hiram and Edwin arble excavated an opening about seven et in diameter and 145 feet long. If they ound pirate treasure, it was never made public. (AAS)

PITESTONE: What may well be the most massive stone wall in New England, rising to eleven feet igh and sixteen and a half feet wide at its peak, was built in the late 1800s in the town of Westminster y Edmund Proctor, a farmer. Reason: to shut out a neighbor, Farwell Morse, who objected to Proc-or's farming on Sundays. Proctor died at seventy-one on November 11, 1890. He and his wife had even sons and a daughter, all given first names beginning with A and middle names beginning with H. ugustus Howard was born in 1845, Alber Hamlin in 1850, Alson Hows in 1852, Alden Herman in 853, Ammer Hale in 1855, Angia Holbrook in 1857, Abbott Herd in 1862, and Amboy Harlem in 864. On the wall is Karen Poikanen, daughter of the owner of the property in the 1950s. (WT&G)

UR LEGGED TREE, BRIDGEWATER, MASS.

FOUR TREES OR ONE? Natural phenomena were much appreciated in early Massachusetts, possibly because they suggested a divine presence to the Bible-oriented inhabitants. Visitors were invariably taken to the scene of this oddity at Bridgewater, shown around 1907. (AAS)

SIAMESE OAKS at Pratt's Junction, Sterling, about 1907. (AAS)

THE BIG ELM in Northampton Meadows, the largest in western Massachusetts when the photograph was taken about 1875, thrilled the heart with its splendor. Despite its impressive girth, the tree was secondary to the famous Rugg Elm in Framingham the largest elm in Massachusetts, which was twenty-five and a half feet in circumference. (AAS)

OLD PHOTOGRAPHS contain little humor. It is almost as if levity was suspect. Yet now and then it is clearly apparent, such as in this scene of a man at wet Medford Pond on October 17, 1869. Triumphant, with dry feet, he has walked upon the waters. Surely he must have been brought to the rock in a boat—but you can't prove it. Or he may have removed his shoes, rolled up his pant legs, and walked to the rock—but you can't prove that, either. All you can do is smile. (AAS)

BOSTON'S WORST DISASTER was the Great Fire of 1872, ruins from it shown here on Milk Street, where 185 firms, most of them in leather, boots, and shoes, were burned out. Note the effect of the fire on the stone pillars. The holocaust began November 9 and was not brought under control until the afternoon of the following day. An epidemic of distemper in horses then raging in Boston considerably reduced the fire-fighting efforts. Nearly a thousand businesses were destroyed with a total value of $75 million.

THE WINTER of 1874-75 was one of the severest in Massachusetts history, with extreme snow and extreme cold, particularly unusual on Cape Cod. The photo shows great blocks of drift ice on Race Point in Provincetown, the outermost land of the Cape. Provincetown was hermetically sealed by a vast ice field over an area of twenty-two miles, grasping in its icy embrace all intermediate shores and havens, wrote historian Samuel Adams Drake. (AAS)

A VISE OF ICE sheaths the fishing schooner *Henry A. Paull* off Provincetown during the dreadful winter of 1875. Flags of distress were displayed in every direction from the masts of crippled vessels that no help could reach. Their hulls, rigging, and tapering spars were so ice-crusted as to resemble ships of glass. As many as twenty signals of distress were counted at one time by the life-saving station. Some of the luckless were crushed and sank to the bottom; others were abandoned by their crews, who had eaten their last crust and burned the bulwarks of their vessels for fuel. The remainder were at length released by the breaking-up of the ice floe, which only relaxed its grip after having held them fast for a month. (AAS)

THE CHICKADEE is the official bird of Massachusetts and one which is willing to brave the natural happenings of the Bay State.

THE CLASSIC ICE STORM of December 1921 in Worcester caused immeasurable damage to trees and telephone and electric lines. For dozens of years a close-up aftermath view of this storm pinching an icy wrap on wires and branches appeared in school geographies. (AAS)

SPRING RAINS POURING into Lynde Brook Reservoir in Leicester could not be contained. On March 31, 1876, at 6 p.m., the dam burst, sending 760 million gallons coursing through a mile long, 100-foot-wide ravine. In five hours the flood wreaked $319,000 in damage. Some prominent citizens of Worcester, to which the reservoir had supplied water since 1865, are looking over the ruins.

[116]   THE WORST DISASTER in its history struck the industrial city of Haverhill on February 17-18, 1882. Ruins of a five-story factory point up the holocaust. The view, taken while the ashes were still smouldering, is looking east. (AAS)

BLOWN ASHORE on Nantucket's sandy beach during a storm, a three-master seems to wait patiently for the ebb tide to run its course. Time: about the turn of the century.

ONE HUNDRED YEARS went up in smoke and 17,450 people were made homeless in ten hours when the Great Chelsea Fire burst out in a heavy gale on the Sunday morning of April 12, 1908. This view shows Chestnut Street from Third, with the Universalist Church and Central Congregational Church in the distance. (AAS)

THE DESOLATION is that of a major fire in Salem on June 25, 1914, which burned out a large and decrepit industrial area. The owners, refusing to rebuild, moved to other communities. (AAS)

THE DEVASTATING HURRICANE that swept into southern New England on September 21, 1938, took eighty-five lives and caused an estimated $100 million in damages, much of it in Massachusetts. Parts of Worcester were literally blasted, reveals this row of large trees knocked down like dominoes. (WT&G)

THE GREAT HURRICANE of 1938, among other caprices of its 100-mile-an-hour wind, left a two-masted fishing dragger stranded on top of a pier in New Bedford. (WT&G)

STAGE SET: ENTER THE WIND. A major tornado—swift, unexpected, dismaying in its intensity—cut an incredible swathe through Massachusetts on June 9, 1953. In Holden, it neatly sheared the entire front from one house without disturbing the contents. Now the world could look in and see one man's family as it lived in six rooms and an attic. (WT&G)

Summer Was the Best Time

THRIFT AND HARD WORK, family matters, and town meetings were serious consumers of the Massachusetts calendar in the old days, but everyone relaxed a little in the summer. Even farmers took time off for cattle fairs or county fairs, and city folks had an array of enticements to draw them away from home on weekends and holidays.

Sunday rides in Boston were a must, often to its public garden where pavilions, bridges, rustic bowers, and the famous swan boats drew crowds seeking fresh air and diversion. There were busy, puffing excursion trains and paddle-wheelers at Martha's Vineyard; breathtaking mountain views to be seen through a telescope; historic monuments to meditate on, or if you were a child, to play tag around.

Dance halls and waltzes ("Take Me Out to the Ball Game"); lighthouses; vaudeville shows; fishing; surreys with fringe on top at Plymouth Rock to take the sightseers around; canoes; strolls along the beach for the sea air and the view; bathing in the ocean in bulky attire (which included bathing shoes if the shore was rocky); goat carts for the children; croquet; camp meetings for religious groups; cottages both modest and grandiose; and picnics in pine groves.

Public parks, which are so much a part of today, became more and more available, meaning that one did not have to go far from home or to a farmer's field for outings or a game of ball. In 1854, Elm Park in Worcester was honored with being the first to have its land bought specifically for a public park.

Some things in the Massachusetts' summers of long ago were just the same as now, except everything was a little less crowded and less used up. Tennis, archery, golf, and gardening haven't changed much, but what were once only for the privileged are available to many today. Last to be mentioned and saved for last on purpose, is that special summer joy of New England sea-shore lovers and feasters—the clambake. The Pilgrims learned it from the Indians of Massachusetts and passed it on.

THIS INNOCENT SCENE was taken at Marblehead Neck in the fashionable summer town of Marblehead on the North Shore, some time in the 1870s. The cottage has been "gussied up" with a canvas awning resting on wooden four-by-fours. Judging from the architecture, particularly the gingerbread, the summer place, as so many in Massachusetts, was built by ship's carpenters. The bowed effect under the roof was often encountered on Cape Cod, but there it was more an integral part of the structure. (AAS)

THIS PLEASANT RURAL SCENE in the 1870s is in Framingham at Lake View Camp Ground. The Victorian structure with its scalloped gingerbread and bird cage is named Cottage Home. Everyone is purposely posing for the camera, including the pair holding croquet mallets. The man has stripped to his vest for the game—but the hat stays. (AAS)

SUMMER SPLENDOR at the Ward house in Stockbridge surrounds an affluent young lady in lace pantaloons seated on her hobby horse. Her sculptured curls are a work of art, and so is her hand-made steed of real horsehide. (AAS)

A YOUNG DRIVER in a goat cart poses at Oak Bluffs, Martha's Vineyard, about 1875. When the last goat cart disappeared would be difficult to track, and even a photograph with working goats is rare. Yet here are the goats, a buggy whip to urge the creatures, and even a reclining dog in a classic pose usually reserved for Dalmatians in old-time fire stations. (AAS)

STUFFED HERRING GULLS in the parlor, oil lamps and genuine bentwood rocker in use, and much more mark the cottage of C. B. Erwin on Ocean Avenue, Oak Bluffs, Martha's Vineyard, about 1880. (AAS)

GAY HEAD LIGHT on Martha's Vineyard about 1880, with a host of summer visitors, up, down, on four feet, and on wheels: First built in 1799, the lighthouse was rebuilt in 1859 with 1,003 prisms of polished crystal which every ten seconds flashed three white beams and one red. (AAS)

THE SURREY with a fringe on top once escorted respectful tourists to Plymouth Rock, then flanked by an ornate granite structure of fearful symmetry. Half of the rock, split by frost in 1775, was removed to the front of Pilgrim Hall for forty-six years, but was rejoined under the canopy erected in 1880. The upper part of the structure contained some bony soil excavated while exploring Cole'e Hill, the first burial ground of the Pilgrims. The ornate edifice was later removed and replaced with a more classic structure. The white paddle-wheel steamer *Gov. Andrew*, at left, was named in honor of Massachusetts Gov. John A. Andrew (1818-1867). (AAS)

AN ARRESTING SIGN at the entrance of the town of Webster testifies to the lake with the longest name in the nation—a constant delight to schoolchildren. The locals called it Lake Webster. Semantic tiffs challenging the authenticity of Lake Chargoggagoggmanchauggagoggchaubunagungamaugg were settled years ago by a renowned scholar, Professor Horsford of Harvard, who said it meant "boundary fishing place." Other accounts say a closer translation from the Nipmuck language is "I fish on my side. You fish on your side. Nobody fish in the middle."

LIVING IT UP beside the sea at Marblehead:
Bathing suits dry on rocks at left. Time:
August 25, 1871. (AAS)

CAREFULLY ARRANGED to fill the camera's eye, with even the picnic basket given a spot at far left, a group of tourists pose on the rocks of Cape Ann near Gloucester, around 1875. The bearded man at left center is holding a long fishingpole. (AAS)

A STIFF GAME OF CROQUET is in progress on the green fronting the Prospect House, a summer resort in lofty Princeton which was popular in the 1800s for its "salubrious air." Interesting is the manner in which the photographer D. C. Osborn overcame the bugaboo of his art—the tendency of the human body to shake—by cleverly utilizing the croquet mallets as canes. The moment that faster films and an improved lens appeared, the photographers dubbed their photographs "instantaneous," as op-. posed to the previous time exposures. (AAS)

THE SCENE IS 1877. At Martha's Vineyard the paddle-wheeler has just come in, discharging its passengers who will board the busy little train with a cowcatcher. It was a joyful, enthusiastic, and patriotic America then with future unlimited. (AAS)

GEM OF MASSACHUSETTS MOUNTAINS is only one of the names given to Mount Holyoke whose trap-rock tip, it was claimed, offered the richest view in New England. On a clear day you could encompass seventy miles, to New Haven and to the highest peaks of Massachusetts. A hotel was opened on Mount Holyoke in 1825, succeeded by two others. Once, earlier, an ample supply of Jamaica and St. Croix rum, Holland gin, and French brandy or cherry cordial was laid in for the visit of Lafayette here, but, behind schedule, he rolled through the town without stopping. Famous guests of the 1800s included Charles Dickens, Jenny Lind, and Nathaniel Hawthorne. A short dramatic railway of 365 feet within 600 feet of incline shot up to the top, but it became a victim, along with the hotel, of the Great Depression in 1936. (AAS)

THE CELEBRATED SWAN BOATS of Boston Public Garden were installed in 1877, designed by "Admiral" Robert Paget and operated by his family for three generations. The bicycle-pedaled craft were enlarged in time with horizontal rows of seats, and became as much an attraction of Boston as the cable cars of San Francisco. This photograph was taken not long after the first boats were installed. (AAS)

SUMMER CAMP MEETINGS, made attractive by the therapeutic and benevolent salt-air climate, began on the island of Martha's Vineyard in 1835 in an area called Wesleyan Grove, the northern part of Edgartown. Thousands attended. The popularity of the resort led to the building of a Methodist Episcopal tabernacle, around which grew a surprising number of small cottages, ornate with architectural gingerbread and fanciful names. "Fairies Abode," shown in about 1877 with a typical, well-dressed group of religious campers, sported a jovial sign: We'll Camp a While in the Wilderness, and Then We're Going Home. The area, which came to be known as Cottage City, petitioned for its own identity and became a township in 1880, but changed its name to Oak Bluffs in 1907. (AAS)

RADIATING BROTHERHOOD and sisterhood, a group of enthusiasts in 1875 attend the old campground of Cottage City on Martha's Vineyard. A dedicated, even smug assurance of being one of the Lord's anointed, is hinted at in the expression of the man with the top hat. (AAS)

THE STEAMER CLAM is considered by many gourmets as among the tastiest of natural foods, a fact known in Massachusetts since the early Indians, who taught the clambake to the Pilgrims, passed on the good word. Pollution, overuse, and disease have nearly decimated the soft-shell clam in the state. This scene shows part of the world's biggest clambake, staged in Plymouth in 1957 by a seafood canner and a Boston radio station. Over six thousand guests gleefully stuffed themselves with 4,800 pints of clam stew, 200 bushels of clams (from Maine), 5,000 lobsters, 6,000 pounds of sweet potatoes, 5,000 ears of corn, 200 watermelons, and 8,000 cups of coffee. (WBZ-Boston)

LENOX IN THE BERKSHIRES boasted seventy-five mansions in 1900 and was one of the richest small towns in the nation, often called the inland Newport. With far less exposure to the public because of its relative seclusion and vast acres of privacy, society passed many pleasant years in gardening, archery, golf, tennis, bob-sledding over the hills, and curling on the ponds. The closing of the social season each September was marked with an event called the Tub Parade. In it, dozens of hand-scrubbed carriages, artfully decorated with flowers grown on the estates of the socialites, rolled through the public streets. An artist from *Harper's* drew the Tub Parade of 1886. The income tax and decline of cheap domestic help brought the spendthrift era in Lenox to a dismaying halt, as it did in Newport, and many shuttered mansions and pseudo-palaces soon became private schools, religious retreats, or other institutions.

THE WINNER snorts up steep Dead Horse Hill in Leicester during an auto race about 1910, thrilling hundreds of spectators. The height took its name for obvious reasons. (WHS)

Main Street, Massachusetts

THE MAIN THOROUGHFARE of almost any Massachusetts city or town is an interesting study in growth patterns. Many began as an earth-packed Indian trail, following the easiest contour from place to place. It was only natural—and much less work—to follow it than to hack and heave primeval trees. Most of the early houses were adjacent to a trail, which in a while became a road for horses and wagons, then a double road when enough traffic justified it. The omnipresent four corners usually had a well for public use and often a trough for horses and cattle and, sometimes, the same water with a bottom trough for dogs, cats, birds, and creatures of the night.

When gas was perfected, modest street lights were installed. Then tracks were laid down for horse-drawn trolleys. The next step was to pave the streets, which put an end to mud, the bane of long skirts; and finally came the miracle of electricity. The automobile accelerated road-paving as nothing else, until only rural byways would be left to remind one of the slower, more-peaceful transportation of yesterday.

[131]

THE QUAINT VILLAGE of Provincetown in about 1838 had most of its houses bordering a single street some two miles long, with a chain of sand hills rising "immediately back of the houses," observed John Warner Barber. "The street is narrow, irregular and has scarcely the appearance of being a carriage road, and the sand is very similar to snow in a driving storm." In his woodcut, Barber pictured the flakes, or frames, on which codfish were dried, and the numerous wind or salt mills by which salt water was raised for evaporation. "So rarely are wheel carriages seen in the place that they are a matter of some curiosity," noted the artist. "A lad, who understood navigating the ocean much better than land carriages, on seeing a man driving a wagon in the place, expressed his surprise at his being able to drive so straight without the assistance of a rudder."

FOUR CORNERS in Marshfield Hills was where everything came together, and most Massachusetts communities had one or more. Often a well was put in the center of it, marking it as a community gathering place. This view of Pleasant Street was taken in the late 1800s. A gas-illuminated light marked the meeting of the roads and also lit up the signposts. The roads had not yet been paved,!, but large, gracious homes and magnificent trees were everywhere. (AAS)

THE MOST HEAVILY developed of Gardner's four compass-point villages was West Gardner, here shown at the turn of the century. This intersection was known as the Square, from the original shape of it. Six streets converge here. (AAS)

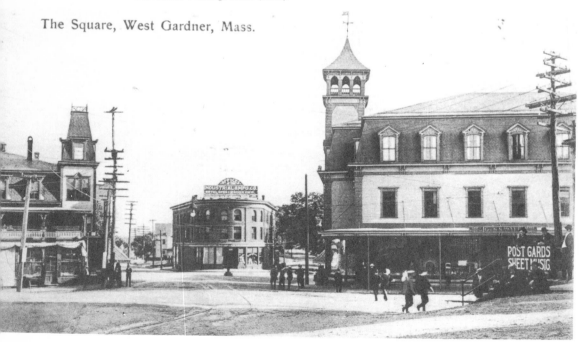

The Square, West Gardner, Mass.

[132]

EAST BROOKFIELD, a typical Massachusetts town, dozes around the turn of the century. The street is unpaved, but water mains and gas lights are installed even though the horse is unaware yet that four wheels can beat four legs. Sign proclaims the livery stable of Issai Lessard, who also rented his own services. In 1926, while drawing a tip-cart loaded with gravel for a bridge, his team backed too closely to the edge, hurling driver, two horses and cart into twenty feet of Lake Lashua. The horses were drowned, but Lessard was rescued.

THE TOWN OF HOLDEN, here shown in earlier days with seven-tier light poles and meandering, rutted roads, grew in fits and starts. It has become a bedroom community for its giant neighbor, the city of Worcester. (AAS)

MAIN STREET in Milford about 1900 shows many men on a cool day indulging in what looks like loitering—an unusual pastime for the work-oriented New Englander of that period. (AAS)

THE GRACIOUS MAIN STREET of Hingham, with its fine shade trees intact, early in 1900. (AAS)

MAIN STREET in Webster about 1903 featured the Grand Sale Shoe Store which sold, not earth shoes, but shoes that were the cheapest on earth. A bicycler in those days could travel down the exact middle of the road. (AAS)

A LOOK EASTWARD on Main Street in Fitchburg about 1903 shows in the distance the tower of the railroad station. Stores with names evoking the glamor of goods available in metropolitan centers such as Boston and New York were beginning to be popular. They suggested imports and the latest fashions. (AAS)

THE SQUARE in Peabody about 1903, with its imposing granite Civil War memorial, built in 1881, rising from the center. (AAS)

MAIN STREET in Melrose in 1904 had what seems today a superabundance of store-front awnings, literally one or more for each establishment. They would have been handy during a rainstorm, but were more likely used only to shield window displays from sun-fading. (AAS)

WATERTOWN'S MAIN STREET is shown here around 1904 as it curves westward. (AAS)

THE MAIN STREET in Chatham on Cape Cod in 1905: The first building at right is the post office, followed by the town barber, whose striped, red and white pole is a throwback to early days when a barber also worked on blood-letting. (AAS)

THE DOMINANT THEME of Main Street in Marlboro in summer 1905 included trolley cars, horses and buggies, and shirt sleeves. The photographer of this scene was able to capture people moving about without blurring them, an indication of the advance to faster film. (AAS)

TOWN HOUSE SQUARE in Salem, which matured earlier due to its prosperity as a seaport: Note the public stanchions for tying horses in the center of the street. Two types of public street transportation had developed by 1905. (AAS)

THE SECOND LARGEST CITY in Massachusetts, Springfield, by 1909 had added a new ingredient, the automobile, to its horses and trolleys. The scene is Main Street, South Springfield. (AAS)

The Seals of Massachusetts

OFFICIAL SEALS became mandatory for all Massachusetts municipalities after April 10, 1899, when the legislature voted: "Within one year from the passage of this act every town not already having a seal shall, by such method as may be adopted by vote of the town at a meeting called for the purpose, establish a seal of the town, which seal shall be in the custody of the town clerk; and any paper or document emanating from any officer or board of a town shall, whenever it seems necessary or desirable, be attested with the town seal."

Many town fathers, uncertain how to delineate their ancient history in such abbreviated form, turned to advice offered in 1817: "The design upon the seal of a city should be unique, that it may not resemble that borne by the seal of any other city. For it is an enduring link between the past and the future. It may bear upon its face an epitome of the city's history, which it carries down to a remote posterity. While books perish and monuments crumble, the seal is among the most imperishable of memorials. . . ."

On the endpapers of this book are seals—including the Great Seal of the Commonwealth of Massachusetts—that represent Massachusetts cities and towns. Nearly all are circular, Most have a pictorial scene showing their finest hour. Massachusetts was heavily influenced by water. As a result, 37 out of 100 municipal seals depict water, ships, fish, or whale. There are 22 showing Indians. Lexington and Concord pridefully reveal their Minutemen. Ipswich had the motto: "The Birthplace of American Independence, 1687," based on a public protest against the oppressive acts of Governor Andros. Provincetown has the motto: "Birthplace of American Liberty," rising from the Pilgrim Compact.

Index